THE CIVIL WAR
SUPPLY CATALOGUE

Published by Crown Publishers, Inc.
201 East 50th Street, New York, New York 10022.
Member of the Crown Publishing Group.

Random House, Inc., New York, Toronto, London, Sydney, Auckland

CROWN is a trademark of Crown Publishers, Inc.

Photo credits on page 201
Quotation on page 68 reprinted by permission of Warner Books, Inc.
from *Soldiers in Blue & Gray* by James I. Robertson.
A version of the Confederate battle flag sidebar appearing on pages 170-172 was originally
published in the April, 1994 issue of *Smithsonian* magazine.
Twelve lines of poetry appearing on page 172 are reprinted with the permission of the University of
North Carolina Press from *Fighting for the Confederacy: The Personal Recollections of General
Edward Porter Alexander* edited by Gary W. Gallagher. Copyright © 1989 by the publisher.

Developed and produced by

Burlington, Vermont
Julie Stillman & Gary Chassman
Design by Stacey Hood

Manufactured in Canada

Library of Congress Cataloging-in-Publication Data

Wellikoff, Alan.
Civil War supply catalogue: a comprehensive sourcebook of
products from the Civil War era available today / Alan Wellikoff.
   p. cm.
Includes bibliographical references and index.
ISBN 0-517-88703-7
1. United States--History--Civil War, 1861-1865--Collectibles-
-Catalogs. 2. United States--History--Civil War. 1861-1865-
-Equipment and supplies-Catalogs. I. Title.
E646.5.W44 1996   96-25328
973.7'074'73--dc20   CIP

ISBN 0-517-88703-7

10 9 8 7 6 5 4 3 2 1

~ To Uncle Eppie ~

THE CIVIL WAR
SUPPLY CATALOGUE

A Comprehensive Sourcebook of Products from the Civil War Era Available Today

ALAN WELLIKOFF

Crown Publishers, Inc.
New York

CONTENTS

Acknowledgments

This book, which discusses the Civil War in material terms, is itself the expression of a lifelong interest in that conflict. The idea, of course, is not to trivialize history, but to show the rich historical lore that lies within what some would dismiss as trivia. Virtually all objects have historical significance, but those made with righteous intent (be they books or bayonet replicas) have a nobility of their own. This they derive from their purpose and design—and from the dedication of their makers.

Recognizing this, I cannot but thank Gary Chassman and Julie Stillman of Verve Editions for their role in the development and production of this sourcebook. Mr. Chassman's exceptional ability to create interest in a book idea no doubt figured in the reception it was given by Crown Publishing's Peter Ginna. Mr. Ginna then placed himself among the best of editors, first by offering the author a drink, and later, news of a book club deal, at just the right moments. As for the editing and production of the catalogue, all must be grateful to Julie Stillman for her ability to expertly fashion this book from a shifting aggregate of text and illustrations. Finally, the book's outstanding design—which improves substantially upon anything previously done for the Historical Supply Catalogue series—is the work of Stacey Hood of Big Eyedea Visual Design.

My gratitude also extends to Frederick Gaede of the Company of Military Historians and Donald Kloster of the Smithsonian Institution for the research assistance they provided, and to Margaret Vining at the Smithsonian and Corrine P. Hudgins of Richmond's Museum of the Confederacy for their ability to overcome bureaucratic inertia

in order to provide historical photographs on short notice. Moreover, certain works on the social and material history of the Civil War were of immeasurable value in providing information used for the historical backgrounds of many of the products that follow. Most notable among these are Francis A. Lord's *Civil War Collector's Encyclopedia* and James I. Robertson Jr.'s excellent 1988 study, *Soldiers in Blue and Gray*.

At times less scholarly but always more practical was the help lent by suppliers who showed that generosity and charm are typical of those who also make excellent replicas. Among these were Second Empire Fine Furniture's Stephen Robert Alexander, Clive A. Babkirk of the House of Kirk, Tinner P.M. Cunningham, Mary LaVenture of Enhancements, Lehman Hardware's Galen Lehman, Philip L. Phillips of Dixie Leather Works, Clint Reynolds at the Confederate Treasury, the Jeweler's Daughter Susan Saum-Wicklein, George Wunderlich of the Wunder Banjo Company, John Burrows at J.R. Burrows & Company, and especially Bob Porter, The Carpetbagger, who graciously put in hours of work to advise on those sutlers, manufacturers, and craftsmen who are considered among the best in replicating specific artifacts.

Warm thanks are due to all below as supportive friends and confederates. Thus, I am grateful to Chris Blair, Alan Rose, and Michael Wellikoff for their fellowship and counsel; to Richard Dennis and George Roussos, whose generosity and unacknowledged technical aid go back a book at least; to Barbara and George Elder for cocktails on the veranda; to E. Scott Johnson for legal counsel; to Kenneth Feigenbaum for insights unavailable elsewhere; to Peg and Ben Coster for their Civil War communiqués; to David Kelly, who addressed the difficulty of shooting flattering publicity photos of the author (and whose great-grandmother rode with Lee—one of the few toddlers to do so); and particularly to Elizabeth Grande, who made this book possible by holding the fort against incoming salvos of unwelcome bosh as it was being written.

While all the above gave their help freely, they do not necessarily share in any of the opinions expressed in the book and have had no bearing on its historical errors, which are exclusively the property of the author.

INTRODUCTION

*The best thing about the future
is that it comes only one day at a time.*

— Abraham Lincoln

During the Civil War, it wasn't possible for a Lincoln to go very fast. Today however, with more horses in an engine bay than Phil Sheridan lost around Richmond, a tour of historic sites can criss-cross the map like shot from opposing batteries. Writing this book set me out on such a journey, driving northward past the rebel flags, Kentucky Fried Chickens, Greek Revival double-wides, and other landmarks of our modern Civil War landscape. Near the Mason-Dixon line, a billboard loomed—portal to the state of Pennsylvania. In gaudy script, it welcomed all who approached with the blithe declaration that "AMERICA STARTS HERE."

This news slowed my progress like a screaming fuzz-buster. Wait a minute, I thought as I read the billboard's message again. Didn't we fight a big, bloody war over that issue?

Evidence that we did can be found everywhere, and especially in bookstores, where the sale of works related to the Civil War buttresses the publishing industry. Paradoxically, as these tomes describe America's singular conflict, they spawn enough controversy to become a part of it themselves. Often, these books are just asking for trouble. They're serious history, examining the war in terms of its slavery versus states' rights origins, and attributing the modern fascination with it to the war's status as a defining national moment. Backed up by months and years of primary research, Civil War books variously speculate on the war's true nature as a bloody rebellion; as the Second American Revolution; as a fight to keep the Union together; as the overreaction to a constitutional claim on independence; or as the last, gory gasp of a slave-holding aristocracy besotted with cavalier pretensions.

Other Civil War books and articles offer more predictable points of view. As I discovered years ago after writing a piece on a Civil War subject, even the most balanced analyses can be made to follow the politically acceptable interpretations imposed by the weeping-Indian, wheelchair-accessible, cumbaya *editorialistas* found at quite the most august publications. As it pertains to the Civil War, this phenomenon tends to be corrosive towards towering figures while it adopts an uncritical view of the horrors of slavery, warfare, states' rights, and resistance to authority.

All such works put me in mind of professional environmentalists, who, while making all the sober, scientific arguments they can for the preservation of the natural world, seem embarrassed to mention its exquisite beauty. While the scientific arguments may be strategic and important, they do not tell the entire story. In such a way, the Civil War is more than the confluence of fierce historical forces. It is also a richly atmospheric drama set within an ornate Victorian proscenium—its decorous and sentimental tableaus alternatively charging with swift combat and collapsing into awful despair. To modern eyes, it is a morality play in which the action is refreshingly dangerous and decisive. Moreover, it is made up of actual events—filled with the valor, lofty language, intrigue, invention, humor, unpredictability, cruelty, and tenderness that no Movie-of-the-Week can muster. Best of all, the Civil War's smoky scenes are set in a far wilder America, one in which the touch of man ends in a quaint Victorian cul-de-sac.

This sourcebook is primarily concerned with this drama's props, which in turn determined the Civil War stories presented. While these stories avoid use of the word "rebel" and celebrate Lincoln, Davis, and Lee, their goal is to afford the reader some small measure of Civil War life in actual—i.e. material—terms. Like the products they describe, the stories strive to be engaging while somehow connecting the Civil War to the present. If they seem too romantic for modern sensibilities, it should be kept in mind that they refer to an era that could be described in just the same way.

The Civil War Supply Catalogue is a compendium of period reproductions selected primarily for the way they conform to originals in their materials, workmanship, and design. While these items are newly minted, they include no Civil War-themed games, beach towels, or other such strictly twentieth-century paraphernalia. They are the same items one could have purchased in the nineteenth century, gathered into a single volume.

Cognizant of the mysteries governing the selection of Civil War artifacts that come to be replicated, this book's chapters and subchapters were determined, in the end, by what Civil War replicas and reproductions were out there. The results obligingly formed themselves into the three main chapters ("Home & Farm," "Campground," and "Field") and suggested the somewhat less obvious subgroupings that have been used.

The products are treated as artifacts, capable of shedding light on some associated bit of history. Indeed, I believe that they do represent a type of artifact—one that not only reflects the past, but simultaneously provides insight into the present day's fascination with it. As the archeologists of replicas, we are given an account of what the modern world thinks of the past by seeing what it chooses to resurrect from it. "Whoever [nowadays] makes a buggy whip," said the humorist Jean Shepherd, "performs a modern act." In this way, the reproduction of an

historic artifact inducts it into contemporary life—not only to claim a part of the past for the present, but to imply that its past hasn't yet ended. This makes the Civil War's replicas partly the stuff of its continuing history.

While the words replica and reproduction are generally used interchangeably to describe copies of antiques, focusing on these items has caused me to make an idiosyncratic distinction between them. As it is used herein, the word *replica* refers to an item copied or replicated from one once made in the past. A *reproduction* differs in that to make it, a company (usually the original company) has resurrected old molds, dies, formulas, patterns, or plans to again produce an item from the original materials. Finally, an item in continual production is made as it always has been ever since the Civil War. An example of this is the cut nails produced by the Tremont Nail Company of Wareham, Massachusetts.

Both reproductions and items in continual manufacture are, by definition, authentic. This leaves replicas as the things to be watched. While the cheap and inaccurate (or "farb," in the reenactor's parlance) replica invariably gives a bad name to this entire body of goods, for each supplier of such merchandise there are others that, out of their devotion to the products and the periods these products represent, make replicas of detailed authenticity. While I've tried to limit the replica entries that follow to the latter, I haven't seen all of the products described

and have been forced to consider what is claimed for them in light of the intuition I've developed while writing this series of catalogues. In addition to authenticity, items were selected on the basis of their historical interest, with those relating to an historic figure or event receiving priority. As a consequence of the above, it should be noted that neither I nor the publisher make any guarantees regarding the quality or authenticity of any of the products described in this sourcebook, nor can we vouch for the reliability of the companies, sutlers, and craftspeople offering them.

As the universe of Civil War replicas is great, it would be impossible for any sourcebook to adequately portray them all. However, as this book repeatedly cites sources for mail-order catalogs containing hundreds of additional period items, it also provides access to this universe. Moreover, as new suppliers offering unique period replicas come along, I hope they will contact me through the publisher so I may consider their wares for future books.

Price and ordering information varies in accordance with the wishes of each supplier, so not all prices are listed. As for those that do appear, they are subject to change, so I recommend that readers use them only to infer current prices and not send any money to the suppliers prior to first contacting them directly. Finally, as most suppliers in this book have small businesses sensitive to the vagaries of the marketplace, their locations, telephone, fax and e-mail numbers and addresses are subject to change without notice, and some may have gone out of business by the time this sourcebook is in readers' hands. At that point, of course, their replicas will be well on the way towards becoming historical artifacts in their own right.

HOME & FARM

"*The human suffering, the loss of life, and above all the loss of many a precious soul that is caused by war—would to god that this war might end with the close of the year and we could all enjoy the blessing of a comfortable house and home one more time. I never knew how to value home until I came into the army.*"

—*Pvt. Constantine A. Hege, of the 48th North Carolina Regiment, in a letter to his parents dated December 18, 1862.*

Harper's Ferry circa 1859

Trees

Let us cross over the river, and rest under the shade of the trees.

—Final words of Thomas Jonathan "Stonewall" Jackson, spoken days after his accidental wounding by one of his men during the Confederate victory at Chancellorsville, May 4, 1863.

Combining the virtues of a Flathead 8 and Motel 6, the old Ford brought me through the night to a point just outside Harper's Ferry. The dawn broke, its air redolent of wood smoke, its wintry sun creeping through the walls of a ruin I'd parked beside in the dark. Somewhere nearby, a train barreled down a mountain cut. About a century had passed since Confederates and abolitionists had launched their disparate attacks from those empty streets. I had cut school, taking off in search of history I'd hoped hadn't fully passed. John Brown, we are here.

I wasn't disappointed. In 1862, Harper's Ferry stood on the frontier of two nations at war. It was a prized fabric, a rich weave of North and South, railway and river valley, forest and Federal arsenal. In 1963, a specter of this fabric could still be made out. As seen from the wheel of my blue business coupe, it waved a sepia shadow above the confluence of the Potomac and Shenandoah Rivers.

Thus was I inducted into the Civil War by the real Harper's Ferry of pre-Park Service days. Attuned to the presence of ghosts, I would later almost see A.P. Hill as he burst over the rise above Burnside Bridge at Antietam. Like a schoolboy Patton, I felt I was at the foot of the bridge when, on the

bloodiest day of the Civil War, Hill and his troops appeared. They had raced all the way up from Harper's Ferry at a full gallop to save Lee's right flank in the battle's waning moments.

Standing nearby was a tree that was the merest sapling when Antietam was fought. More importantly, the sycamore that trembled beside Burnside Bridge in 1862 and towered above it in 1963, is still there today—one of the august, living veterans of the War Between the States.

Famous & Historic Trees has introduced biology into what is usually meant by the term "historic reproduction." Its inventory contains the seedlings of more than thirty trees with narrative significance to the Civil War. These trees—the actual

This photograph, taken soon after the Battle of Antietam, shows the immature Antietam sycamore at bottom center.

offspring of historic, Civil War parents—are divided into two categories: The first, or "Witness Trees," are those that grow on battlefields or other important sites (as does the Antietam sycamore), and appear in wartime photographs, scouting reports or battlefield sketches. Second are the "Battlefield Trees," the issue of hardwoods described as standing "at locations that have important Civil War significance." Among the former (and in addition to the Antietam sycamore) are progeny of the "Brompton White Oak," witness to Burnside's debacle at Fredericksburg, Virginia; of the red oak that stands atop Henry Hill, where Gen. Jackson positioned his troops during the First Battle of Bull Run and earned his "Stonewall" sobriquet; of the "Wilson's Creek Chinkapin Oak" that witnessed the death of Nathaniel Lyon, the first Union general to be felled in the war; of the "Gaines' Mill White Oak"; of a Southern magnolia from Andersonville

prison; of the "Gettysburg Address Honey Locust"; of the catalpa that stands on the lawn of "Chaltham," Union headquarters during the bloody battle of Fredericksburg, Virginia; of the white oaks that sheltered Pickett's troops just before his charge at Gettysburg. Battlefield trees include seedlings from a "Manassas Mimosa," a "Shiloh Silver Maple," a Southern red oak from Kennesaw Mountain, an "Appomattox Courthouse Sycamore," and an American sycamore and chestnut oak from the birthplace of Robert E. Lee.

Other categories of Famous & Historic Trees comprise presidential trees (including the offspring of several trees witness to the life of Abraham Lincoln), trees of the American Revolution, trees of "America's Exceptional Women" (with a "Harriet Beecher Stowe White Ash" and "Clara Barton's

Trees"), and trees from Walden Pond, America's artists, Native American history, American inventors, African-Americans (look for a white oak seedling from a tree once belonging to Frederick Douglass), and many more.

As if the work of Famous & Historic Trees were not praiseworthy enough, it is sponsored by American Forests, an organization founded in 1875 and described in their catalog as "the nation's oldest nonprofit citizens' conservation group." In addition to planting America's Historic Forest, American Forests has affiliated with the Civil War Trust (a battlefield-preservation society) to produce the Civil War seedlings. One-third of the purchase price of these go toward furthering the planting and preservation work of both organizations.

Complete instructions for the timely planting and care of all trees by region are included with your purchase.

Price: Civil War trees, $35 each.

Literature available.

Famous & Historic Trees
8555 Plummer Road
Jacksonville, FL 32219
Phone: 800-320-TREE
Fax: 800 264 6869

Address your contributions to:

American Forests
8555 Plummer Road
Jacksonville, FL 32219
904-765-0727

The Civil War Trust
1225 Eye Street, N.W.
Suite 401
Washington, D.C. 20005
Phone: 202-326-8420
Fax: 202-408-5679

House Plans

It's said to have been General Ulysses S. Grant's view of Port Gibson, Mississippi that it was "too pretty to burn". Of course, Grant may have found the town as fair as he did because—fighting his way towards Vicksburg in May of 1863—he passed through the place at dawn. The previous night, Confederate Gen. John S. Bowen had withdrawn through Port Gibson in an effort to avoid being outflanked by Grant. Deftly retreating through moonlight that made the town appear all the more a stage set, Bowen paused only to destroy the bridges that spanned the bayou and streams lying to its north.

Grant's crepuscular arrival found the port populated by long shadows. The general determined that he needed to construct a bridge across the south fork of Bayou Pierre beyond the town, so he assigned a detail commandeered by a staff officer named James Wilson. Whatever regard Grant had for Port Gibson's comely architecture was necessarily forgotten when Wilson seized all the bridge-building materials he required from nearby homes. These he razed and cannibalized to present Grant with a bridge described as a continuous raft some 170 feet long.

At the further expense of Port Gibson's building stock, this 12-foot-wide span also featured a luxury of siderails, corduroy approaches, and abutments.

The nearby plantation known as Windsor was fortunate to be spared destruction by Col. Wilson's crowbars. Built by 600 slaves at a cost of $175,000, the mansion was erected in 1860, its four stories crowned by an observatory from which the Mississippi River could be seen. Prior to Grant's Vicksburg campaign, the house was used as a Confederate observation

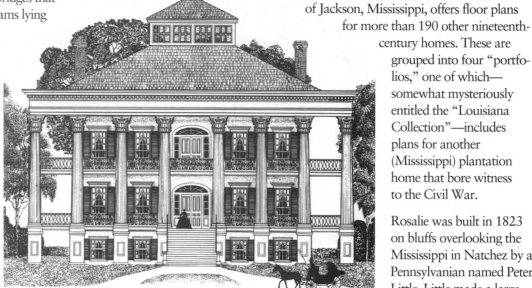

Windsor Plantation

post; with the advent of Union occupation, it served as a military hospital. Sadly, the destruction that Grant would not impose was wrought by a house fire in 1890. Today, all that remains of the mansion that was once a landmark for Mark Twain and other Mississippi riverboat pilots, are twenty-three stately columns.

The house plans for your rebuilding of Windsor show a house measuring 87 by 92 feet, and containing 8,328 square feet of floor space. In addition, Historical Replications of Jackson, Mississippi, offers floor plans for more than 190 other nineteenth-century homes. These are grouped into four "portfolios," one of which—somewhat mysteriously entitled the "Louisiana Collection"—includes plans for another (Mississippi) plantation home that bore witness to the Civil War.

Rosalie was built in 1823 on bluffs overlooking the Mississippi in Natchez by a Pennsylvanian named Peter Little. Little made a large fortune in Southern cotton and lumber, and during the occupation of Natchez, his home served as Union Army headquarters. Measuring 58 feet wide by 80 feet deep, Rosalie contains 6,254 square feet overall. Historical Replications' updated plans for the two-story home feature a "graceful staircase [that] rises to a wide landing."

Prices: A complete set of blueprints containing foundation plans, detailed floor plans, exterior elevations, interior elevations, window and door schedules, building cross sections, framing diagrams, and energy-saving details costs $800 for Windsor and $575 for Rosalie respectively. Packages of five- and eight-set working drawings, and mirror-reverse sets, are available for an additional cost.

Four portfolios, "Classic Cottages," "Colonial Heritage," "Louisiana Collection," and "Victorians and Farm Houses" are $16 apiece. Any two portfolios cost $28; any three, $40; and all four are available for $48.

Historical Replications, Inc.
P.O Box 13529, Dept. CW
Jackson, MS 39236
Phone: 800-426-5628
Fax: 601-956-3288

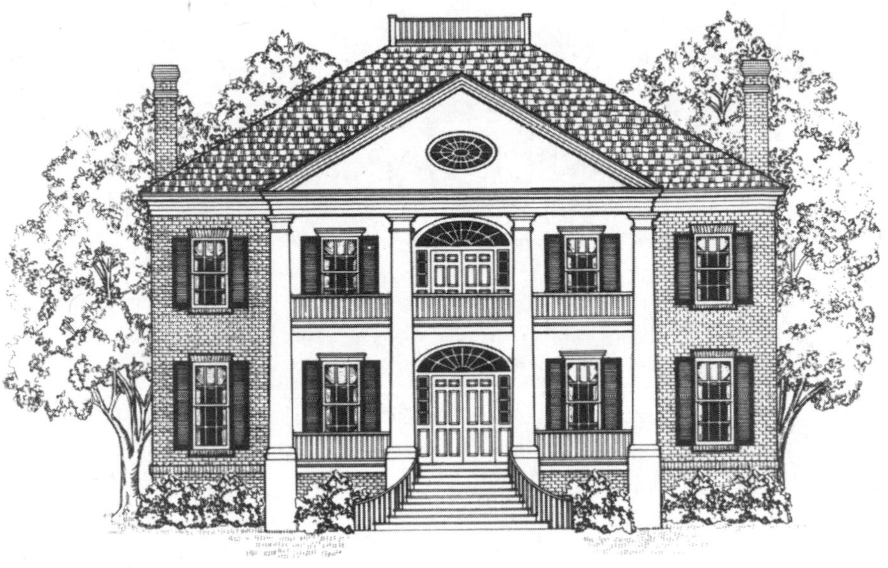

Rosalie

Cut Nails

Fastening the 1790s to the 1880s, cut nails connect the age of handwrought iron nails to today's mass-produced wire varieties. Since 1812 the Tremont Nail Company has been producing cut nails by a process in which a machine-driven blade slices them from a flat piece of steel. This results in a four-sided fastener that tapers towards the head. The taper and machine-made head reflect innovations made around 1810 and 1815 respectively.

Anticipating the fate of the Union, the Tremont Nail Company's first factory was consumed by fire in 1860. To supply the war effort, the nail company carried on operations from a warehouse in a neighboring town.

Cut nails are still routinely used in the working of masonry and (when galvanized) for shipbuilding. Inevitably, they are also used in the restoration of antiques and old buildings. As such, Tremont Nail's fasteners have been driven into projects at Old Sturbridge Village, Colonial Williamsburg, the Harper's Ferry National Monument, Old Bethpage Village Restoration, and other historic sites. Several types of nails are available for every type of restoration.

Free catalog available.

Tremont Nail Company
8 Elm Street, P.O. Box 111
Wareham, MA 02571
Phone: 508-295-0038

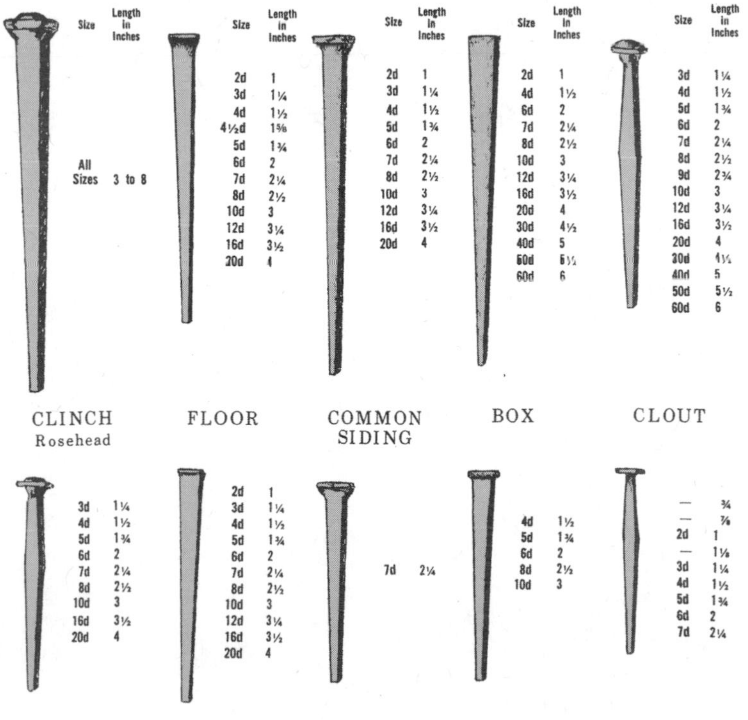

CUT SPIKE

Size	Length in Inches
All Sizes	3 to 8

MASONRY

Size	Length in Inches
2d	1
3d	1¼
4d	1½
4½d	1⅝
5d	1¾
6d	2
7d	2¼
8d	2½
10d	3
12d	3¼
16d	3½
20d	4

COMMON

Size	Length in Inches
2d	1
3d	1¼
4d	1½
5d	1¾
6d	2
7d	2¼
8d	2½
10d	3
12d	3¼
16d	3½
20d	4

FOUNDRY

Size	Length in Inches
2d	1
4d	1½
6d	2
7d	2¼
8d	2½
10d	3
12d	3¼
16d	3½
20d	4
30d	4½
40d	5
50d	5½
60d	6

BOAT

Size	Length in Inches
3d	1¼
4d	1½
5d	1¾
6d	2
7d	2¼
8d	2½
9d	2¾
10d	3
12d	3¼
16d	3½
20d	4
30d	4½
40d	5
50d	5½
60d	6

CLINCH Rosehead

3d	1¼
4d	1½
5d	1¾
6d	2
7d	2¼
8d	2½
10d	3
16d	3½
20d	4

FLOOR

2d	1
3d	1¼
4d	1½
5d	1¾
6d	2
7d	2¼
8d	2½
10d	3
12d	3¼
16d	3½
20d	4

COMMON SIDING

7d	2¼

BOX

4d	1½
5d	1¾
6d	2
8d	2½
10d	3

CLOUT

—	¾
—	⅞
2d	1
—	1⅛
3d	1¼
4d	1½
5d	1¾
6d	2
7d	2¼

Jefferson Davis, U.S.A.

A past (and blessedly forsaken) press release issued by the Chadsworth company took pains to point out that its president, Jeff Davis, shared the name of "a famous Confederate General." Wondering if this wasn't something more than a perfunctory demotion of Jefferson Davis the famous Confederate president by some beauty-academy grad, we looked into the matter. What we learned was that while a Civil War general named Jeff Davis did exist, he was neither a Confederate nor all that famous.

There was this one incident, however.

Jefferson Columbus Davis was a Union brigadier who saw action in the Mexican War and at Fort Sumter. In September of 1862 Davis went to Louisville, where he became involved in the defense of that city against Confederate Gen. Kirby Smith. This brought Davis into violent conflict with his superior, Major Gen. William "Bull" Nelson, the 300-pound commander of the Army of Kentucky. A friend of Lincoln's, Nelson was said to possess even more pomposity than physical presence—but girth and gall both would be felled by Davis in a fit of pique.

Accounts vary, but it certainly all began after Nelson, bristling over the clash of their personalities, ordered Davis from his department. The brigadier went grudgingly, but later confronted Nelson in the Galt House, which was Gen. Don Carlos Buell's headquarters for the Louisville campaign. During their escalating fight, Nelson dismissed Davis as an "insolent puppy," to which the latter responded by directing a wadded-up calling card into his tormentor's face. The commander answered this challenge with a swing of his canvass-ham fist, knocking Davis back. Momentarily triumphant, Nelson then mounted the hotel's staircase to steam towards Gen. Buell's room and demand of a passerby if he had "seen that damned insolent scoundrel" insult him. Nelson had just reached Buell's threshold when he heard his name called from behind. Turning around, he saw Jefferson Davis standing at the top of the stairs pointing a hastily-borrowed pistol right at him.

continued on page 21...

Greek & Roman Columns

As befits any marriage, the union of America's colonies took place with something old on hand. As architects of a new republic, the founders were drawn to ancient Greece as a model, and went so far as to propose that the Greek language replace English as the national tongue. Of course none of this Grecophilia was intended to slight Rome, particularly for a country that saw itself as the manifest conqueror of a continent; but Greece gave America a chance to proclaim herself heir to elements of the classicism and democracy that European culture revered but had lost.

In this, the architects of the Republic were succeeded by the architects of buildings, and it wasn't very long before the Cincinnatis, Philadelphias, Athenses, Spartas, and Corinths emerging from wilderness replaced their rude cabins with little Grecian temples. The columns of these were decorated with alabaster cornstalks and tobacco leaves—Hellenized flora that rooted well in the soil of the antebellum South. There, in addition to a classical icon of culture, authority, and gentility, ancient Greece offered a venerable justification for slavery. This made Greek Revival architecture into something of a political statement—one that succored the "peculiar institution" of slavery, while at the same time providing an atmosphere wherein free yeomen could assume heroic stature amid America's templed hills.

As Roger G. Kennedy writes in his book, *Greek Revival America*, this architectural style—redolent as it was of peace, rationality, and nationhood—ended with Appomattox. Like the founding fathers' Union itself, Greek Revivalism was killed by the Civil War. "With its solemn rectilinear precincts bounded by the emphasis of columns," Kennedy sees Greek Revivalism as a proclamation that rational Americans might solve their problems without resorting to war. But "when order had collapsed into bloodshed," he claims, "it was impossible to reuse the same symbols."

You might disagree. Greek Revivalism was, by definition, an American exercise in nostalgia. As such, it was an early chapter in a book, dear reader, still being perused by you. How fitting therefore that the pillars of Greek (and Roman) Revivalism are being resurrected today by a Southern company, and one both founded and chaired by a man named Jeff Davis.

Chadsworth's process of authentically replicating the dimensions of their products is perhaps the most exacting of any manufacturer in this book. The columns, which are available in any size, emerge from designs that are computer-generated from original specifications formulated by the Italian Renaissance architect Giacomo Barozzi da Vignola in 1563. Once the style is perfected, the columns are hand-finished from high-grade lumber. In 1994, Chadsworth's began producing columns from non-deteriorating material called PolyStone™.

Free flyer available.

Chadsworth's 1.800.Columns
P.O. Box 2618
Wilmington, NC 28402
Phone: 800-COLUMNS
Fax: 910-763-3191

Jeff Davis U.S.A., continued

The larger figure unwisely responded with an advance upon the smaller one. Before firing, Davis warned the mountainous Kentuckian not to take another step. "I have been basely murdered," Nelson announced to those who hoisted him onto a nearby bed. He died there within a half-hour.

Buell immediately placed Davis under arrest, a circumstance that might have made him wish that he had followed the example of his Confederate opposite—Pvt. Abraham Lincoln of the 1st Virginia Cavalry—and deserted. However, as presidential orders arrived that morning to relieve Buell of his command, the arrest was itself arrested for a time. Eventually, the matter was dropped like its victim, enshrining in Davis the status of a man with whom it was wise not to trifle. Thus endowed, he went on to serve in Alaska and the Modoc War.

Lincoln Parlor Stove

Less a Civil War replica than a testament to Lincoln's marketability on the verge of the next century, this stove's design is nonetheless based on those of a century past. As such, it has a large, non-airtight firebox, a double-lidded cook top and mica windows—all crowned by a chrome-plated finial.

Specifications: Overall size, 40 inches high by 25 inches wide by 23 inches deep. Log length, 18 inches; flue size, 6 inches, oval; (side-mounted) load door size, 14 inches high by 9 inches wide; average burn time, 4 hours; maximum output, approximately 40,000 Btu; weight, 231 pounds.

Price: $349.

"Non-Electric, 'Good Neighbor' Heritage Catalog," $3 ($4 Canada).

Lehman's
One Lehman Circle
P.O. Box 41
Kidron, OH 44636
Phone: 216-857-5757
Fax: 216-857-5785

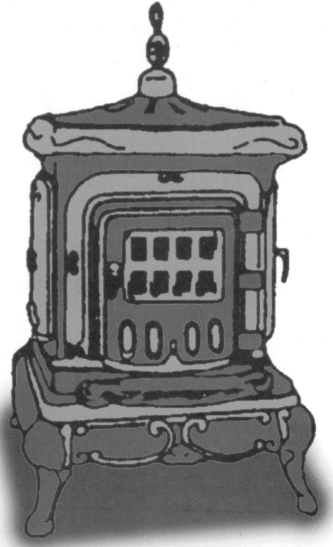

Jefferson Davis Bed

A presidential bed of doubtful authenticity in regular, queen, and king sizes.

Prices:
$3,160; $3,305; and $3,595 respectively.

Lincoln Rocker

From the Confederacy's first capital, a "Lincoln rocker" handcarved in Honduran mahogany.

Dimensions: Height, 45 inches, width, 23 inches; depth, 36 inches.

Price: $975.

Catalog of Victorian furniture available.

Heirloom Reproductions
1834 W. Fifth Street
Montgomery, AL 36106-1516
Phone: 334-263-3511
Fax: 334-263-3313
Order line: 800-288-1513

Charleston Battery Bench

*If the people over the river had behaved themselves,
I could not have done what I have.*

—Abraham Lincoln

Although it won the siege that began the War Between the States, the Confederacy lost the waltz that preceded it.

Before the rebel capture of Fort Sumter on April 14, 1861, Lincoln's advisors were confident that he would order its small garrison evacuated. They expected that a Federal withdrawal would keep Dixie's hound-dogs of war from hunting for awhile, and recognized that the fort's location in Charleston's sea channel would make its capture by the South inevitable anyway. Lincoln's cabinet strongly favored abandoning Sumter, and as they viewed the new President as little more than a mid-chart Darwinian specimen, figured that he'd obediently cede the fort to the secessionists. But Lincoln had different plans: With his April 6 dispatch of an armed naval expedition to reinforce Sumter, the President confounded advisors and adversaries alike by putting the latter in the position of either backing down from their threats against the fort, or launching an attack upon it. Such an offensive would not only mark the Confederacy as aggressor, but would, as Jefferson Davis was warned by his Secretary of State, Robert Toombs, "wantonly strike a hornet's nest which extends from mountains to ocean," resulting in "a civil war greater than any the world has yet seen."

Few men were as steadfast as Davis when a principle was involved and—believing that Lincoln's armada would cause the world to see the U.S. as assailant whoever shot first—the Confederate president would not retreat. So despite Toombs' dread prophesy, Davis issued an order on the 10th for General P.G.T. Beauregard to demand that federal troops quit Sumter, and, if refused, "to proceed in such a manner as you may determine to reduce it."

Gen. Beauregard sent out two soldiers in a rowboat to meet with Major Robert Anderson, Sumter's commander. Anderson, who had been Beauregard's instructor at West Point, sorrowfully declined the demands of his former student's emissaries; and saying, "If we do not meet again in this world, I hope we meet again in the next," saw them away from the wharf. Within hours, the "honor" of firing the first shot of the war would fall to one of these soldiers—a Virginian named Roger Pryor. Days before, Pryor had stood on a Charleston balcony exhorting Carolinians to "strike a blow" for the Confederacy; but when the lanyard to that blow was offered, he declined with emotion, saying that he could not fire the first gun.

Fort Sumter under bombardment.

Less squeamish and more "sesech" (secessionist) was Edmund Ruffin, an old-line rebel and crusty newspaper editor. It was no doubt with a curmudgeonly display of brio that Ruffin touched off the Civil War's first mortar at 4:30 on the morning of the 12th. As seen from Charleson's shoreline Battery, the shell traced a crimson ellipse through the city's sea and sky before bursting above Sumter and into a fusillade of four years' duration.

The Charleston Battery Bench is made from the original mold pattern of those benches lining the Battery in the mid-1800s. "It is a very authentic piece of Charleston history," says Andrew Slotin, Director of Charleston Battery Bench, Inc. "given that its manufacture has been continuous since the middle part of the nineteenth-century and is still being made *exactly* as was done some hundred plus years ago." The bench uses Carolina cypress dip-painted in the traditionally-dark Charleston green, and depicts in its heavyweight castings the flora and fauna indigenous to the state during its nineteenth-century period of secessionist fervor. The maker asks that you note that, as it is with New Orleans, ironwork is closely attached to Charleston's history. Hence the bench's "inverted parrot, fox and hound, and extensive use of a foliate motif overall."

Dimensions: Available in 30-inch single, 6 foot and 8 foot double benches. All are 28 inches high and 21 inches deep.

Prices: $199.50, $399.50, and $469.50 respectively.

Free brochure available.

Geo. C. Birlant & Company
191 King Street
Charleston, SC 29401
Phone: 803-722-3842
Fax: 803-722-3846

Garden Furniture

We have to detail a good many men to protect the gardens.

— Union Col. and Civil War diarist Elisha Hunt Rhodes

Concerned as he was with the possibility of food shortages, Col. Rhodes was not discussing the kind of gardens that sprout extravagantly curlicued metal benches. For such gardens however, the Moultrie Manufacturing Company's "Old South Collection" has aluminum replicas of cast-iron furniture from the antebellum South. As it is the only collection specifically identified as being copied from 1846 originals, the "Baronet Grouping" is of particular interest. Consisting of a settee, chair and bench, the group's master patterns are the same as those of the benches used in the White House garden.

Measurements: Settee: length, 58 inches; height, 35 inches; seat depth, 15½ inches; overall depth, 18 inches; height to seat, 17 inches. Chair: height, 33½ inches; width, 23½ inches front, 16 inches, back; depth, 14½ inches. Bench: height, 16 inches; width, 44¼ inches; depth, 15 inches.

Prices: Settee, $1,484.41; Chair, $965.63; Bench, $1,060.30.

Catalog of cast-aluminum furniture replicas available.

Moultrie Manufacturing Company
P.O. Drawer 1179
1403 Highway 133 South
Moultrie, GA 31776-1179
Phone: 800-841-8674

Wooden-Frame Lanterns

As a Civil War camp lantern would often consist of a candle mounted in the neck of a bayonet that had been jabbed into a wall, the Kentwood Sutlery's "Civil War-Era" lanterns replicate domestic types.

Three types of these wooden-framed lanterns are available: a 13-inch-high by 6-inch-square model with a brass cover; the same with a door replacing the candle base; and a 6-sided double candle type, 13 inches high by 16 inches wide by 6 inches deep, and incorporating three reflecting mirrors.

Catalog of "Civil War-Era Items," 75¢.

Kentwood Sutlery and Manufacturing
P.O. Box 88201
Kentwood, MI 49518
Phone: 616-531-7645

1860 Clock

A recreation of the E.N. Welch Company's 1860 Patti model is available in the same solid walnut case as the Connecticut-built original. Above a cast brass pendulum, its baked-enamel dial is marked by Roman numerals and flanked with four ornate Victorian columns. All are surmounted by a precisely turned rail.

Dimensions: Height, 20 inches; width, 12 inches; depth, 5½ inches; shipped weight, 29 pounds.

Price: $270.

Catalog of "Goods in Endless Variety for Man and Beast," $4.

Cumberland General Store
#1 Highway 68
Crossville, TN 38555
Fax: 615-456-1211
Order line: 800-334-4640

Carpets

There is a prodigious cry of 'On to Richmond' among the carpet-knights of our city.

—George B. McClellan, *McClellan's Own Story*, 1862.

During the Civil War, "carpet-knights" were State and National Guardsmen, who in Gen. George B. McClellan's eyes, constituted a Savonnerie-hugging horde that "loathed to shed blood" in the cause they so belligerently espoused.

Reproductions of the carpets these commandos may have trod are carried by J.R. Burrows & Company. The Massachusetts firm's carpets are woven in an 1850s English mill using documented historical patterns that date to the late eighteenth century.

Ironically, none of McClellan's carpets (McClellan was nicknamed the "Virginia Creeper" for his own loathing to get off the deep pile during the Peninsula Campaign, see "McClellan Saddles," page 156) are represented in the J.R. Burrows line. However, patterns from the company's collection were selected as floor coverings for the historic homes of General William Tecumseh Sherman, Judge David Davis (Lincoln's first appointee to the Supreme Court), and Union generals George Crook, Grenville Dodge and Ulysses S. Grant—whose Galena, Illinois home uses the "Baroque Cartouche" design shown here. J.R. Burrows' carpets also cover floors in the President Andrew Johnson National Historic Site and the Lincoln-Tallman House—a Janesville, Wisconsin home that sheltered the future president for a period in the 1850s.

The J.R. Burrows company also offers a line of scrupulously researched and manufactured period wallpapers and lace panels.

Catalog and samples available, $5.

J.R. Burrows & Company
P. O. Box 522
393 Union Street
Rockland, MA 02370
Phone: 617-982-1812
Fax: 617-982-1636

Ingrain Carpets

Sarah's carpet was common ingrain, neither pretty nor new.

—Marion Harland, pseud. Mary V. (Hawes) Terhune, *Husks*, 1863.

Perhaps Sarah's ingrain carpet was thirty years old, dating back to the time in the 1830s when power looms began to make them available. According to historian Jack Larkin, about 25 percent of this period's parlor floors were covered with what then were, despite Mrs. Harland's later disdain, woolen symbols of gentility. Aspiring families made do with rag rugs and painted canvas floorcloths.

Ingrain carpets are defined in textile dictionaries as flat-woven carpets made from yarn that has been dyed prior to weaving. Having researched "document pieces of carpet analyzed by the Philadelphia College of Textiles" Family Heir-Loom Weavers has accurately duplicated the weight and twist of mid-nineteenth-century yarns. Their ingrain carpet weft is spun according to their specifications by "the oldest carpet yarn spinner in the United States" (their warp—a finer yarn than weft—is a blend of 80 percent worsted wool and 20 percent nylon, double the strength of that used in the nineteenth century). Family Heir-Loom's patterns are all replications of original designs.

The Civil War history of Family Heir-Loom's ingrain carpets includes their use in such historic sites as Wheatland, the home of President James Buchanan in Lancaster, Pennsylvania; at Abraham Lincoln's home in Springfield, Illinois, where the Maple Leaf and Geometric and Floral designs fill five rooms; and in the McLean House in Appomattox, Virginia, where a McLean-pattern carpet replicates the one trod by U.S. Grant and Robert E. Lee when the latter surrendered the Army of Northern Virginia.

Prices: Geometric and Floral, a two-ply 1830-1840 antebellum ingrain carpet design, 36 inches wide, $97 per yard; Maple Leaf, a two-ply 1850-1880 Victorian carpet design, 54 inches wide, $125 per yard; McLean House, a three-ply 1850-1880 Victorian carpet design, 35 inches wide, $135 per yard.

Family Heir-Loom offers eight designs of 36-inch wide ingrain carpet for stairs. The document pieces they have designed replicate ones ranging in year from 1810 to 1910.

Information on replica ingrain carpets, woven coverlets, and denim and shirting materials available.

Family Heir-Loom Weavers
775 Meadowview Drive
Red Lion, PA 17356
Phone: 717-246-2431
or 717-244-5921

The Ancient's Greek Revival: Lincoln's Springfield Illinois home.
Lincoln Home National Historic Site.

Wallpaper

A house divided against itself cannot stand.

—Abraham Lincoln

The Springfield, Illinois, home that Mary Todd and Abraham Lincoln moved into in 1844 was by no means divided. However, in 1850 the future president was obliged to build a retaining wall to keep his Greek Revival place from coming apart. The building is still there. Unfortunately, the analogy would not hold up as well.

The home on Eighth and Jackson Streets stood one and a half stories high, had a frame of rough-sawed oak held together by wooden pegs and handwrought nails. Pine was used for the interior trim and doors, and the floors were made from oaken planks. Here, three of the Lincolns' four sons were born: Edward Baker, William Wallace, and Thomas—the first dying in the house in 1850, aged five years.

In 1856, with Springfield becoming citified by railroad links to Chicago and St. Louis, Mrs. Lincoln undertook some major improvements to the house. For $1,300 she had builders add a top floor containing four rooms, transforming the dwelling into a two story building. The upstairs woodwork was given an artificial walnut stain to match the decor below, and two false fireplaces were built into the upper bedrooms to house Franklin stoves.

Mt. Diablo Handprints of Benicia, California, offers a replication of the 1850s English block-print wallpaper used in the Lincolns' parlor, and the French block-print used in their bedroom. In keeping with the firm's policy of offering wallpapers that they have replicated on commission from historic homes, museums, and societies, both of these were first reproduced for the Lincoln Home National Historic Site in Springfield.

To recreate its historical wallpapers, Mt. Diablo uses whatever documentation is available to define the original's design elements. The final product is screened by hand with water-based inks. Their collection includes "Frost Grape" an 1853 machine-print wallpaper that dressed the walls of Stonewall Jackson's Winchester, Virginia headquarters. Jackson was not so preoccupied with the Shenandoah Valley campaign that the paper, which shows gold-highlit grape vines, escaped his notice. "The walls are decorated with elegant gilt paper," he wrote his wife, Mary Anna Morrison Jackson, in a successful effort to induce her to come and spend the winter with him, "I don't remember to have ever seen more beautiful papering."

Finally, there are the Grevemberg Scenic, the Grevemberg Lattice and the Widow Clarke Stripe patterns, all replications of Louisiana originals that are notable for their having been torn down and used for newsprint during the war. All, according to historical design researcher John Burrows, "are among the most accurate Civil War wallpaper reproductions available."

Prices: Lincoln Bedroom, $54 per 7-yard roll; Lincoln Parlor, $51 per 7-yard roll; Frost Grape, $45 per 6-yard roll; Grevemburg Scenic, $45 per 7-yard roll; Grevemberg Lattice, $45 per 5-yard roll; Widow Clarke Stripe, $45 per 7-yard roll.

Jackson in an 1862 portrait made during the Shenandoah Campaign in which the Confederate general admired the "Frost Grape" wallpaper pattern (left).

Other wallpapers in the Mt. Diablo catalog represent historic designs from the 1840s to the 1940s and feature Victorian, Anglo-Japanese, and Arts and Crafts papers.

Illustrated catalog obtainable.

Mt. Diablo Handprints
940 Tyler Street # 56
P.O. Box 726
Benicia, CA 94510
Phone: 707-745-3388
Fax: 707-745-1726

LADIES' CLOTHING

Whether due to the influence of French couturiers or the sentimentalist spirit of the times, the period preceding the Civil War is marked by more gaiety in fashion than had been seen earlier in the century. Beneath brightly colored jackets and skirts, both the social and whalebone corsets encumbering womanhood were loosened. Now it was acceptable for skirts to be coyly raised for a glimpse at the confusion of colored crinolines, embroidered petticoats, and white silk or cotton stockings that previously rustled in darkness.

Of course Boston's puritanism forbade such caprices, and Philadelphia's Quaker heritage maintained complete austerity. However, after watching female passersby parade their multi-hued parasols, lace gloves, and fluttering ostrich feathers, Charles Dickens claimed that ten minutes' sightseeing on New York's Broadway presented more colors than could ten years spent anywhere else.

With a small sampling of its replica nineteenth-century clothing and uniforms, R&K Sutlery of Lincoln, Illinois, could costume the above paragraphs thus:

Fashion print from a mid-nineteenth century edition of Le Bon Ton

1860s Jacket and Skirt

Available with matching reticule, $89.95 and higher. Bolero jacket with skirt and matching reticule, $79.95 and higher.

Corset

A "basic 1863" version, made of cotton drill and available in colors with lace trimmings, $52.50 for sizes 20 and below.

Cotton Stockings

Available in black and beige in addition to white, $6.

Lace Gloves

Also available crocheted, $7.

Parasols

Despite their already being caged in bonnets, parasols provided even greater protection for the pale feminine complexions prized at mid-century. These parasols have "a plain, solid body," a 33-inch-diameter wire frame, and a wooden tip and handle. Obtainable in white, red, blue, pink, and Dickensian black. With plain edged panels, $10; ruffled, $15; with 2-inch fringe (black and white only), $18.

Ostrich Plumes

$2.

Catalog of replica mid-nineteenth-century clothing and uniforms available.

R&K Sutlery
1015 1200th Street, Lincoln, IL 62656
Phone: 217-732-8844

Ball Gown

Tightly-fitted bodice is designed with a V-shaped neckline, cut to ride just off the shoulder. It has a deep point at the center front and is laced down the center back. Its short sleeves puff above the elbow, and its full skirt fits loosely over a hoop of up to 140-inches in circumference. A variety of colored fabrics, trimmings, and embellishments can be chosen.

From Les Modes Parisiennes, *May 1857*

Gettysburg's Civil War Lady's Things offers customers a great deal of latitude in the design and construction of its clothing, underpinnings, and accessories. With a small part of these, it could outfit Dickens' passage down Broadway with the following items:

Woolen Cloak

For traveling and formal occasions. The long-length cloak is fully lined and features a hood large enough to cover a bonnet.

Ornamental Petticoat

As were those seen by Dickens, this colored petticoat was meant to be glimpsed. It is patterned and trimmed with scallops, braids, and velvet bands, and incorporates flounces to help hold the skirt out. Over and under the hoop petticoats also available.

Evening Stockings

In cotton, wool or silk with a "clockwork" design.

Chinese Parasol

A white-paper parasol with cane ribs for seaside, or informal country use. Authentically replicated umbrellas, and varieties of silk, long-handled parasols also obtainable.

Catalog, $4.

Gettysburg's Civil War Lady's Things
230 Steinwehr Avenue, Rear Building
Gettysburg, PA 17325
Phone: 717-334-9712
Fax: 717-334-7482
Internet Address: www.servantandco.com

Pagoda Skirt

A box, or knife-pleated skirt, describing an elliptical "footprint" and having a shape dependent on that of the crinoline beneath. As with most dress skirts of this period, the pagoda skirt had a woolen braid sewn onto the hem to protect it from wear. A gored-panel pyramid skirt is also available.

The Mariann Day Dress

A military-style dress, the bodice and pagoda sleeves of which are trimmed with tassels and braid. The sleeves are also "neatened" on the inside bottom edge with runching. The skirt is plain and has a twill tape hem protector. As with all Mrs. Martin's clothing, no velcro, zippers, or zigzag stitching are used.

Price: $300.

The Catherine Ball Gown

An evening dress documented to 1861, its skirt is trimmed with bands of velvet put on in deep, bow-decorated points. The bodice is available with either a deeply pointed or rounded waistline. Sleeves are puffed and worn under epaulettes. Mrs. Martin's ball gowns are laced up the back through handworked eyelets.

Price: Cost for labor on ball gowns begins at $350 with the final price determined by the fabric and trim used.

Day Caps

Made in different styles of the 1860s, with varying fabric and trim.

Catalog of "historically-correct, custom-made, period clothing from 1850 to 1865 for the discriminating woman," $4.50.

Martin's Mercantile
4566 Oakhurst Drive
Sylvania, OH 43560-1736
Phone & Fax: 419-474-2093

Bonnets

From Enhancement Costume Supply's Mary LaVenture:

"The bonnet's origins can be seen in styles popular during the Georgian period. During the first few decades of the nineteenth century, the bonnet took hold and there were many variations. From a style called the 'Kiss-Me-if-You-Can' bonnet (named such for its unusually long brim) to the popular capote and poke bonnets, the large bonnets of the early century were scaled down during the middle part of the century. The 'bavolet'— a short skirt or frill attached to the back of the crown covering the neck—was a standard feature on most bonnets of this time. Another addition, in the form of a second brim attached to shield the sun, was called the 'uglie.'"

All such bonnets and attachments are available from Enhancements. In addition to the bavolet and "uglie" bonnets, the firm's Old Fashioned, Settler, and Sun bonnets are shown.

Prices: Range from $9 - $79.

Catalog of hats, bonnet frames, millinery and corset-making supplies, hoops, bustles, panniers, stockings, collars, wigs, nets, hat pins, and more, $3.

Enhancements Costume Supply
P.O. Box 8604
Anaheim, CA 92812-0604
Fax: 714-638-4545

Sun bonnet

Old Fashioned bonnet

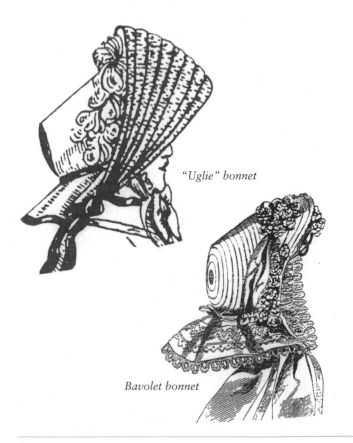

"Uglie" bonnet

Bavolet bonnet

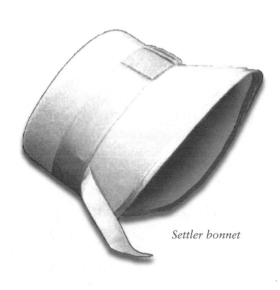

Settler bonnet

Ladies' Crinoline or Hoop Petticoats

From Enhancements' Mary LaVenture:

"By the 1850s, skirts had continued to grow in volume and some type of skirt support was needed. An alternative to forever increasing the number of petticoats was found in the use of a foundation garment strengthened with whalebone or metal. In the latter part of the decade, the former was replaced with "watch-spring" steel. The dome-shaped hoops formed with these materials would eventually become scaled down as they evolved into the 1870s bustle."

Enhancements Costume Supply has a variety of hoops in several colors and sizes. They also stock a cage crinoline as well as bustles and panniers.

Prices range from $36 to $103, depending on number of bones and type of material used.

Catalog of hats, bonnet frames, millinery and corset-making supplies, stockings, collars, wigs, nets, hat pins, and more, $3.

Enhancements Costume Supply
P.O. Box 8604
Anaheim, CA 92812-0604
Fax: 714-638-4545

Bone hoop

Sansflectum crinoline

Cage crinoline

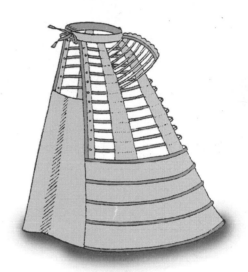

Crinolette

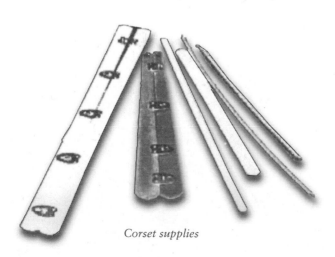

Corset supplies

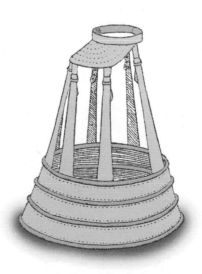

Scarlet flannel crinoline

Ladies' Underpinnings

Driven by the clatter of sewing machines, the ever-increasing layers of women's undergarments provided a measure of the drama taking place in 1850s fashion. Early photographs document that by the advent of the Civil War, ladies' dresses had become enormous hives of rustling crinoline, bustle, petticoats, and other stiffening.

Martin's Mercantile offers a complete line of replica nineteenth century ladies undergarments, including drawers, petticoats, a chemise, corset, corset cover, and camisole.

Catalog of "historically-correct, custom-made, period clothing from 1850 to 1865 for the discriminating woman," $4.50

Martin's Mercantile
4566 Oakhurst Drive
Sylvania, OH 43560-1736
Phone & Fax: 419-474-2093

Chemise

Camisole

Petticoat

Split-crotch drawers

Cage crinoline with patent draw string

Cage crinoline

Cotton crinoline

Crinoline with horsehair flounce

Gentlemen's Apparel

Men's French fashions for 1865; a sporty tweed suit with a high-crowned hard felt hat; a formal tail coat with a tall shiny top hat; semiformal frock coat with a gray top hat.

Derby

From Enhancements' Mary LaVenture:

"The Bowler family was responsible for making a hat style for Locke's of St. James in the 1850s. The bowler was a hard, round-crowned hat, less formal than a top hat. In the 1860s, when the Earl of Derby chose to wear the hat to the races, word quickly spread to the United States, where it became popular with all classes of men."

Price: "Morefelt Derby," in black, gray, or brown, $36.

Catalog of hats, bonnet frames, millinery and corset-making supplies, hoops, bustles, panniers, stockings, collars, wigs, nets, hat pins, and more, $3.

Top Hats

Can you get in here, sir? That's *the Department of State, sir!*

—Robert Augustus Toombs, the first Confederate Secretary of State, in response to an office seeker, while pointing to his hat.

History does not record whether or not the Confederate Department of State described in this encounter was housed in a top hat or other head covering. However, considering Toombs' bark, we'd guess it was the former—a headpiece devised by a hatter in the 1790s and described as " a tall structure ... calculated to frighten ... people."

If frightening people was Lincoln's purpose in donning the even taller "stovepipe" top hat, it didn't have the intended effect. This can be inferred from two things said to the stovepiped Lincoln. The first, "You need more dignity," a suggestion made by a New York supporter, may or may not have included a reference to the president's high-rise headgear; while the second, "Get down, you damn fool, before you get shot," a remonstration to tall-target Lincoln as he stood atop Washington's besieged Fort Stevens (and directly under his silken black sequoia), almost certainly did. Fort Stevens was part of Washington's defenses probed by forces under Confederate Gen. Jubal A. Early before he aban-

Stovepipe

doned his plan to seize the U.S. capital and president in July 1864. This exhortation—or something like it—has often been attributed to then Lieutenant Oliver Wendell Holmes, Jr.. However, the quote was not claimed by the Supreme Court Justice until some 60 years after the event, and is generally believed to be the words of another soldier.

During the nineteenth century many styles of top hats were available with varying crown heights, brim widths, and shapes. In addition to the stovepipes, bell crowns and Wellingtons traced a line of descent from their riot-provoking 1790s ancestor. Enhancements offers all these plus an "1860s Topper" and a "Collapsible Satin High Hat," which was perfected during the 1830s and 1840s by the Parisian hatmaker Antoine Gibus.

Prices range from $24 for the "Topper" in black, gray, and brown to $175 for the "Collapsible Satin High Hat" in black (a collapsible satin hat in white is available for $225.) The 1860s Topper and Stovepipe hats are available for $82 and $28 respectively.

Enhancements Costume Supply
P.O. Box 8604
Anaheim, CA 92812-0604
Fax: 714-638-4545

1860s Topper

Bell Crown Top Hat

A dress hat worn from the mid-1850s through the turn of the twentieth century. Made from beaver fur felt, with leather sweatband, lining, and tippet.

Price: $100.

Brochure and price list available.

Clearwater Hat Company
Box 202
Newnata, AR 72680
Phone: 501-746-4324

Detachable Collars

The Gibson-Lee company began producing disposable collars in 1864, when Southern control of cotton cut off all but paper varieties from Northern production. Today, according to company literature, they use the original 1864 machines to produce period collars including those made of cloth laminated to paper stock.

Gibson-Lee Corporation
78 Stone Place
Melrose, MA 02176
Phone: 617-662-6025

Clothing items similar to those found in this chapter also obtainable from:

Greta Cunningham
402 East Main Street
Madison, IN 47250
Phone: 812-273-4193

Lincoln Shawl

Black woolen shawls were often worn in the mid-nineteenth-century. Abraham Lincoln was fond of the double shawl and is often depicted wearing one. Amazon Drygoods' version is 100 percent wool and measures 72 by 144 inches. Fold it first into a 72-inch square, and then a triangle.

Catalogs of "Authentic Patterns From the Past," and "Shoes and Boots, $5 a piece.

Amazon Drygoods
2218 E. 11th Street
Davenport, IA 52803-3760
Phone: 319-322-6800
Fax: 319-322-4003
Order Line: 800-798-7979

Footwear

An assortment of late Victorian footwear is obtainable.

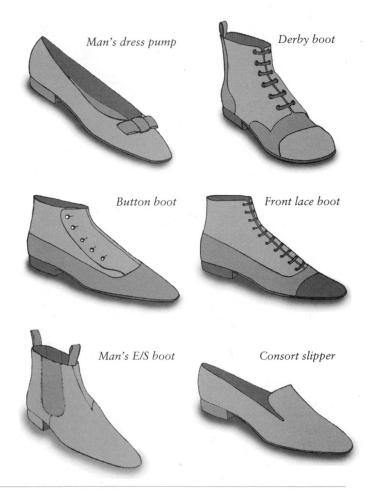

Man's dress pump

Derby boot

Button boot

Front lace boot

Man's E/S boot

Consort slipper

Ladies' Clothing Patterns

Past Patterns has been in the business of manufacturing historical clothing patterns since 1979, a time in history when men's shirt collars had grown big enough to risk antitrust action. During the intervening years, the firm has accumulated a bit of history itself—and with it an enviable reputation for authenticity. For its primary sources, Past Patterns uses original garments, the pattern blocks from nineteenth-century magazines, and pattern drafting systems and original tailor's manuals from the nineteenth and twentieth centuries. The company then enlists the aid of computer design programs to ensure a level of accuracy that has made Past Patterns the apparent choice of many reenactors.

Paletot

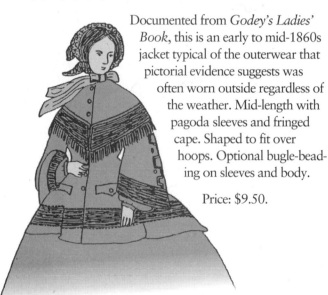

Documented from *Godey's Ladies' Book*, this is an early to mid-1860s jacket typical of the outerwear that pictorial evidence suggests was often worn outside regardless of the weather. Mid-length with pagoda sleeves and fringed cape. Shaped to fit over hoops. Optional bugle-beading on sleeves and body.

Price: $9.50.

Fishu

Documented from *Graham's Illustrated Magazine*, this late 1850s to mid-1860s light wrap is made of stiff net over which is placed puffings of tulle highlighted with ribbon.

Price: $7.50.

Visiting Dress

An early to mid-1860s dress copied from one in the Cincinnati Art Museum. It has a fitted bodice with front darts and a single, fitted back piece.

Price: $9.50.

Garibaldi Dress

Also from an example in *Godey's*, this dress has a bloused bodice with waistband and buttons on the "man's side."

Price: $7.50.

Catalog of Civil War-era patterns available.

Great American Pattern Emporium
341 Mooreland Avenue
Harrodsburg, KY 40330
Phone: 606-734-0028

1850 to 1867 Gathered Bodice

The post-1840 movement from "romanticism" to "sentimentalism" in women's dress described by Robert Lacour-Gayet in his book, *Everyday Life in the United States Before the Civil War*, imparted a "languishing air" to the feminine figure partly through the use of full, long sleeves paired with fitted bodices. Past Patterns' illustration of its 1850-1867 Gathered Bodice, shows a loose-fitting bodice with the peg-top sleeves that were fashionable in the 1860s. The bodice front is fastened with hooks and eyes.

Price: Multisized tissue pattern, sizes 10-20, $10.

1860s Ball Gown Bodice

Reflecting the region's more established society, Southern balls afforded attendees great informality. By contrast, New England affairs tended to be corseted by social constraint, while New York parties were lavish and spirited.

At a New York ball given in seven magnificently furnished rooms by Lucretia Mott for the Prince de Joinville, the mistress wore a pink crepe de chine dress embellished with "'scrolls and a lace flounce." The affair lasted until three a.m., when the diamond-bodiced Mrs. Mott invited the Prince and his retinue to sit down to supper with her family. At another New York party given for Charles Dickens, the costumes included all the dress necessary for *tableaux vivants* of scenes from his works to be presented before the celebrated author.

Past Patterns' 1860 ball gown pattern incorporates French seams to achieve the proper sleek-sculpted look from neck to waist.

Price: Multisized blue-line, $10.

1850s to Late 1860s Garibaldi Shirt

From 1859 to 1862 Giuseppe Garibaldi led his volunteer army of "Red Shirts" through a brilliant series of military campaigns against Austria in the cause of Italian unification. In support of his guerrilla movement—or out of admiration for the figure cut by their dropped shoulders, loose sleeves and tight bodices—Garibaldi shirts anticipated Mao caps and the jackets Ike and Nehru by about a century when they became popular here in the late 1850s.

Price: Multisized tissue pattern, $10.

1860 to 1870s Homestead Dress

While prosecuting the Civil War, in 1862 the U.S. government yielded to the popular agitation for land in the West by passing the Homestead Act. Under the terms of this law, homesteaders would become entitled to 160 acres of land after living on the quarter section allotted to them for a period of five years. This property would be freely granted, except for a small fee. While a boon to western farmers, the Homestead Act was notoriously exploited by land promoters who faked settlement of the land, fraudulently gaining title to it and reselling it. That is their story. These are the dresses they wore.

Price: Multisized tissue pattern sizes 10-20, $13. Cotton calico or linen material.

Patterns for these additional Civil War-era articles of clothing are available: 1830s to 1860s stick-out petticoat, 1850s to 1860s chemises, 1850s to 1860s drawers and petticoat, 1850s to 1860s wrapper, late 1850s to mid-1860s hoop skirt, 1860s sack and petticoat, 1862 to 1867 Madame Roy skirt-supporting corset, 1863 Dayton skirt-supporting corset, Federal-issue men's trousers and a Victorian sunbonnet.

1860 to 1870 Stay or Corset

Women of this period "decided to be seductive by emphasizing their independence," the French social historian Lacour-Gayet maintains. In the culture of this period, such sexy sovereignty favored the female body's near-immobilization. Protected from any contact by semirigid corsets, women "continued to delight in making martyrs of themselves."

Past Patterns' 1860 to 1870 stay, or corset follows one patented in 1863. It fastens with a center front clasp and adjusts with laces in the back.

Prices: Pattern, $7; kit, $39.

A pattern for a more cylindrical 1840s to 1880s corset is also available for $7, $29 for the kit.

"Patterns for Vintage Clothing," a catalog of early nineteenth-century, Edwardian, Flapper, and Depression-era clothing patterns obtainable, $3.

Past Patterns
P.O. Box 7587
Grand Rapids,
MI 49510-7587
Phone: 616-245-9456
Fax: 616-245-3584

Gentlemen's Clothing Patterns

1860s Men's Evening Suit

A suit with a fitted frock coat, the lapels of which extend sharply toward the shoulders. The clothes are formfitting, with a fully lined vest cut high with a rounded collar. The tails move into a double pleat at the center back. The trousers are of moderate width in cut. Some knowledge of tailoring is recommended.

1860s Men's Cape

A three-quarter-length cape with a stand-up collar. It features a triangular section that is set onto the top, with the point of the triangle falling to the center back of the cape.

Catalogs of "Authentic Patterns From the Past," and "Shoes and Boots," $5 apiece.

Amazon Drygoods
2218 E. 11th Street
Davenport, IA 52803-3760
Phone: 319-322-6800
Fax: 319-322-4003
Order Line: 800-798-7979

1800 to 1890s Men's Drawers

Most of the boys had never worn drawers and some did not know what they were for and some of the old soldiers who are here told them they were for an extra uniform to be worn on parade and they half believed it.

— Theodore Frelinghuysen Upson of the 100th Indiana in a letter home, 1 August, 1862.

These patterns allow for short and long lengths, the latter typical of drawers worn during the 1860s.

Price: Multisized tissue pattern, waist sizes 32-42, $10.

"Patterns for Vintage Clothing," a catalog of early nineteenth-century, Edwardian, Flapper, and Depression-era clothing patterns obtainable, $3.

Past Patterns
P.O. Box 7587
Grand Rapids, MI 49510
Phone: 616-245-9456
Fax: 616-245-3584

Men's Dress Shirt

When you come home you shall have some shirts to make up for Charles.

—Jane Austen

Shirt with underarm gussets, shoulder reinforcements, and shaped armholes. Decorated front insert with separate collar pattern included. From *Godey's Lady's Book*.

Price: $7.50.

Men's Civilian Sack Coat

Beginning in the 1850s, the vogue in men's coats was for them to be short, loose, shapeless, and made of tweed or serge. By the 1860s, this outfit, albeit finer, neater and better fitting—was widely accepted as informal wear by broad classes of men. The Great American Pattern Emporium's version is an appropriately short, loose coat with no waist seam. It has a small center back vent and slit, exterior pockets.

Price: $9.50.

Men's Civilian Shirt

Underarm gussets, shoulder reinforcements, front button slit with packet. Cuffed sleeve and optional breast pockets.

Price: $7.50.

Men's Single-Breasted Civilian Frock Coat

Also copied from an example in a private collection, this frock coat has exterior pockets and two piece sleeves with wide elbows. The roll-down collar comes with tips on how to get it to lay flat.

Price: $7.50.

Catalog of Civil-War era patterns available.

Great American Pattern Emporium
341 Mooreland Avenue
Harrodsburg, KY 40330
Phone: 606-734-0028

CHILDREN'S CLOTHING PATTERNS

Children's patterns including girls' aprons, gored and muslin frocks, and boat necked yoke and high-Garibaldi dresses. Also a boy's French blouse and buttoned suit. All are circa 1860, with the exception of the boy's French blouse, which is documented to 1864.

Prices: Muslin frock and boy's French blouse patterns, $10. All others, $12.

Catalog of "historically-correct, custom-made, period clothing from 1850 to 1865 for the discriminating woman," $4.50.

Martin's Mercantile
4566 Oakhurst Drive
Sylvania, OH 43560-1736
Phone & Fax: 419-474-2093

Muslin frock

Gored frock

High Garibaldi dress

Aprons

Boy's French blouse

Boat neck yoke dress

Boy's buttoned suit

Boys' Civil War Patterns

Civil War patterns for boys include a military-issue-style shirt, a great coat, shell and frock jackets, a Union Army sack coat, and a Confederate regimental coat. Girls' patterns include a Zouave suit and a Garibaldi blouse.

Catalog of "Authentic Patterns From the Past," $5.

Amazon Drygoods
2218 E. 11th Street
Davenport, IA 52803-3760
Phone: 319-322-6800
Fax: 319-322-4003
Order Line: 800-798-7979

Boy's jacket

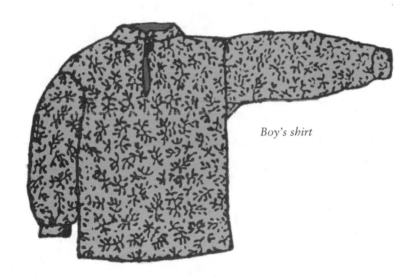

Boy's shirt

Boy's coat

JEWELRY

While Purple Hearts were being won in the field, 1860s jewelry such as crosses, lockets, and cameos decorated the home front breasts that patiently abided, laden with the sentimental regard for family, country, and religion that characterized the era.

The "Jeweler's Daughter," Susan Saum-Wicklein, is the great-granddaughter of Hampton Saum, a watch regulator for the Western Maryland Railroad late in the last century. Mr. Saum opened a small shop near the rail yard that sold jewelry nearly four-score years before Mrs. Saum-Wicklein joined what had become the family business. In creating The Jeweler's Daughter, Saum-Wicklein sought "to address the needs of Civil War reenactors and living historians for appropriate … and quality jewelry appointments." What follows is a sample of her period jewelry.

Victorian Chatelaines

From the French meaning the mistress of a chateau, the chatelaine is a kind of nineteenth-century women's tool belt. Worn at the waist, they usually sported large, decorative medallions from which several hanging chains carried household objects such as scissors. Fancy chatelaines such as the one depicted were suitable for evening wear.

The Jeweler's Daughter offers a variety of Victorian chatelaines and their appropriate attachments. All are cast in sterling silver.

Price: Completed chatelaine sets range from $113.95 to $152.95.

Victorian Earrings

Patterned after a style worn in the 1860s, these earrings are available in both black onyx and goldstone and are set on gold-filled wires.

Price: $21.95.

Watch Chains

Used by both ladies and gentlemen to carry timepieces, replicas of these are available in a variety of historical styles. Available in gold-filled sterling silver or 14-karat gold, the watch chains can be crafted to meet personal specifications.

Prices: $29.95 and up.

Video catalog and price list, $5.

Emily Mason Bread Riot Ring

Emily Virginia Mason was a hospital matron who oversaw convalescents from the Georgia divisions at Camp Wynder, near Richmond. Late in the war, a rumor that the hospital steward had stolen their rations led 200 of her Georgian wards to stage a bread riot. They tore down the camp's bakery and mauled its baker until Miss Mason stepped in. Chastised into apparent remorse, several of the rioters offered themselves up for incarceration on behalf of the entire group—while others pooled their meager resources to send the

steward (whom they had nearly hanged) into Richmond to buy Miss Mason a small token of their affection. The steward returned with a ring that the Georgians dutifully presented to the matron, who they said had "conquered them."

Under agreement with Richmond's Museum of the Confederacy, which holds the original in its collection, The Jeweler's Daughter has replicated the "bread riot ring." It is available in 10-karat yellow gold, and will be sized to your specification.

Price: $129.95.

Masonic Ring

In 1826, William Morgan of Batavia, New York, became so exercised over a dispute with his fellow Freemasons that he left the order and wrote a book revealing its secret rituals. Soon after, he was kidnapped and never seen again, although a body "tentatively" thought to be his later washed up onto the shores of Lake Ontario.

Perhaps the beached William Morgan would have been more easily identified had he been wearing his Masonic ring. This unfortunate incident fed the sentiment that resulted in the formation of an Anti-Masonic Party late in the 1820s. Although their presidential candidate was soundly defeated in the election of 1832, anti-Masonic views were held during the course of the nineteenth century. This atmosphere undoubtedly strengthened the fraternal bond existing among Freemasons, and encouraged the many instances when they rose above the sectional differences of the Civil War.

A poignant example of this is the succor given the mortally wounded Confederate Brigadier General Louis Armistead by his brother Mason, Federal Captain Henry Bingham, after the former fell, mortally wounded, on the barrel of a Union cannon, at the high water mark of Pickett's Charge.

The Jeweler's Daughter's Masonic ring was produced after consultation with the order's historians to ensure accuracy that includes the use of Masonic symbols appropriate to the mid-nineteenth century.

Available in 10, 14, or 18 karat gold. Identify ring size when ordering, as an additional fee will be charged for sizes larger than 12.

Prices: 10 karats, $229.95; 14 karats, $339.95; 18 karats, $589.95

The Jeweler's Daughter
2-4 West Washington Street
Hagerstown, MD 21740
Phone: 301-733-3200
Fax: 301-733-5076

Long before the business and political opportunists known as "carpetbaggers" headed south to exploit the situation created by the Reconstruction Act of 1867, carpetbags were a common sight. They began to appear in 1840, six years following issuance of the U.S. patent for the ingrain carpet power loom; and were seen with increased frequency during the 1850s, when the railroads opened travel to those unlikely to have expensive luggage. With the 1870s however, Reconstruction had brought with it so unseemly a class of opportunists, that the bag's reputation was tarnished and its popularity waned. In time, the word carpetbag became so kindred to "scoundrel" that in 1884 the Kingston, New Mexico, Clipper would remark: "An effort is being made to remove more of the jobbers, bloodsucks, and renegade carpet-bag scrubs from our territory."

If after that characterization you still want one, Bob Porter of Middletown, Virginia produces a line of carpetbags the authenticity of which have been refined by years of work with Civil War reenactors. A Falstaff of grand good will, Mr. Porter notes that his carpetbags and haversacks were "carried by the stars" in the CBS mini-series "Queen," and in the films "Tombstone" and "Gettysburg."

Authentic carpetbag

Authentic Metal-Frame Carpetbag

Had Confederate Gen. Robert E. Lee won at Gettysburg in July of 1863, history might now record that his army went on to occupy Philadelphia, and — if that didn't result in peace negotiations — even New York. But Lee lost Gettysburg, and according to historian D.S. Freeman in his book *Lee's Lieutenants*, it was because "Stonewall" Jackson "is not here."

In the present tense that Freeman uses to describe him, Jackson is a man of "contrasts so complete that he appears one day a Presbyterian deacon … and the next a reincarnated Joshua. He lives by the New Testament and fights by the Old." Jackson was also an ingenious tactician, and his Shenandoah Valley campaign ranks with the most brilliant in history.

Another of Stonewall's sobriquets, "Old Blue Light," was not a description of a secessionist Sinatra, but a reference to the incandescent quality that the general's eyes took on in battle. This was evident at Chancellorsville, where Jackson's tactical genius handed Lee his greatest victory. Unfortunately, it was in that same fight where Jackson was wounded by one of his own men. On his deathbed days later, he issued commands from a combat-fraught delirium. "Order A.P. Hill to prepare for action! Pass the infantry to the front…" Then, suddenly at peace, he countermanded the orders and, smiling, expired with the words: "Let us cross over the river and rest under the shade of the trees."

Travelling bags

Patterned after one possibly owned by Jackson while he was a professor at the Virginia Military Institute, this steel-framed carpetbag was the most popular style in use both during and after the war. It has a wooden bottom with brass studs, a muslin lining, leather handles, and an old-fashioned lock. Outside, the fabric is heavy upholstery velvet with the look and feel of old carpet.

Dimensions: 20 inches long by 14 inches high by 6½ inches wide.

Price: $155.

Separate large and small travelling carpetbags, and replica nineteenth-century trunks, haversacks, and purses are also obtainable.

Free catalog.

The Carpetbagger
7805 Main Street
Middletown, VA 22645
Phone: 540-869-7732

Jenny Lind Trunk

From 1850 to 1852, "Swedish Nightingale" Jenny Lind gave 150 concerts throughout the United States under the direction of impresario P.T. Barnum, her chief admirer. Other wealthy devotees paid up to $225 a seat to attend these events, while still others were satisfied by christening varieties of carriages, houses, fruit (see Jenny Lind Melons p. 80) and luggage with the diva's name.

The outside of this hourglass-shaped trunk is upholstered with top-grain cowhide, while a heavier leather reinforces the outside edges, which are studded by several hundred hand-set, brass tacks. The trunk has heavy leather handles on either end and brass feet to set it off the ground. Its top contains a lidded compartment that, consistent with

the originals, has a lithograph glued to its panel.

Dimensions: 12 inches wide by 13 inches high, 18½ inches across the front, with a 4½ -inch high lid compartment.

Price: $434.50.

Travel, steamer and leather coach trunks also available.

Catalog of "'Hard-To-Find' 19th Century Military Goods & Reproduction Living History Accessories," $6 within the U.S., $10 abroad.

Dixie Leather Works
306 N. 7th Street
Paducah, KY 42001
Phone: 502-442-1058
Fax: 502-442-1049
Order Line: 800-888-5183

Jenny Lind, circa 1850

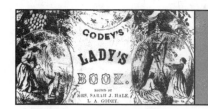
BOOKS

In keeping with the mission of this sourcebook, all the books that follow are facsimiles of old editions about the Civil War published either during it or in the decades after its occurrence. While the best facsimile editions use the cover designs, binding methods, and materials found on the initial printing, reprints generally reshoot and publish the original book's pages.

The Broadfoot Publishing Company is a respected publisher of Civil War titles, including many biographical and autobiographical facsimile editions.

General Lee

by Fitzhugh Lee

This reprint of an 1894 edition of the biography of Robert E. Lee was written by his nephew, Fitzhugh (himself a Confederate cavalry general who was almost dismissed from West Point while his uncle was superintendent there). The book includes many of Robert E. Lee's letters not available elsewhere. This edition has a 31 page introduction with notes by Civil War historian Gary Gallagher, including "the fullest autobiographical sketch of Fitz Lee to date."

General Lee runs 473 pages and includes a frontispiece, portrait, an index and 3 maps. Gray cloth, measuring 6 by 9 inches

Price: $30.

The Last 90 Days of the War

by Cornelia Phillips Spencer

A reprint of the 1866 edition containing the observations of an "intelligent and discerning" North Carolina woman. *The Last 90 Days of the War*'s 323 pages includes a frontispiece and index. The book is bound with brown cloth and measures 5 by 7 inches.

Price: $30.

The Southern Bivouac

edited by Gary Gallagher

Not exactly the facsimile edition of a book, *The Southern Bivouac* is a six-volume compendium reprinting this "Monthly Literary and Historical Magazine" published by the Kentucky branch of the Southern Historical Society between 1882 and 1887. As described by *The Encyclopedia of Southern History*, "The publication included historical papers read before the association, short stories about the Civil War, [and] sketches of soldiers distinguished in the war."

The Southern Bivouac contains more than 3,200 pages, including many steel engravings, maps, and portraits.

Price: $300 prepaid for all six volumes, or $55 monthly for each in succession.

Bethel to Sharpsburg

by Daniel Harvey Hill, Jr.

This two-volume set reprint of an original 1926 edition tells the Civil War story of North Carolina's Confederate troops, with emphasis on their military operations. In addition, there is much information on the Army of Northern Virginia, blockade running, and the occupation of North Carolina.

Volume I is 444 pages, including 7 illustrations, 1 map and an index. Volume II is 477 pages with 8 illustrations and an index. Both volumes are gray cloth, measuring 6 by 9 inches.

Price: $60.

Lt. General Jubal Anderson Early C.S.A.: Autobiographical Sketch and Narrative of the War Between the States

by Lt. Gen. Jubal A. Early

While living in Canada after the war, Early wrote *A Memoir of the Last Year of the War for Independence in the C.S.A. (1866)*, which he later expanded into this work, first published in 1912. This edition is a reprint of that now-rare volume, with an introduction by Gary Gallagher.

Lt. Gen. Jubal Anderson Early is 524 pages, with a frontispiece, 13 illustrations, 11 maps and an index. It is bound in brown cloth and measures 6 inches by 9 inches.

Price: $35.

Lee and Longstreet at High Tide

by Helen D. Longstreet

Gen. James Longstreet mistakenly thought that his superior, Lee, shared his belief that the Pennsylvania invasion that ended with the Battle of Gettysburg was a tactical defensive rather than a strategic offensive. His resulting reluctance to attack on the second day of Gettysburg—and his slowness to organize Pickett's Charge on the third—exposed him to savage criticism from Southerners after the war. This reprint of a 1905 book provides a justification of Longstreet's conduct, and adds weight to the assertion of Lee's biographer D.S. Freeman that the commander of the Army of Northern Virginia "never gave any intimation that he considered Longstreet's failure at Gettysburg more than the error of a good soldier."

Lee and Longstreet at High Tide is 406 pages long, with a frontispiece, 14 illustrations, 3 maps and an index. It is bound in yellow cloth and measures 6 by 9 inches.

Price: $30.

Catalog of Civil War books available.

Broadfoot Publishing Company
1907 Buena Vista Circle
Wilmington, NC 28405
Phone: 910-686-4816
Fax: 910-686-4379
Order Line: 800-537-5243

The Lost Cause

by Edward Alfred Pollard

The reprint of an 1866 book by the wartime editor of the *Daily Richmond Examiner*. The book is ably written, describing the Civil War from a Southern perspective. It is unfortunately a poor-quality reproduction, reprinting the original pages.

Price: $17.98.

Gramercy Books
40 Englehard Avenue
Avenel, NJ 07001
Phone: 908-827-2700

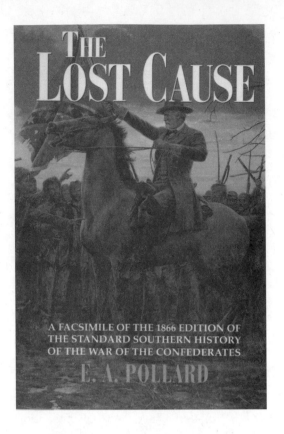

Photographic Views of Sherman's Campaign

by George N. Barnard

An 80-page reprint of a landmark 1866 volume containing 61 plates of Union Gen. William Tecumseh Sherman's campaigns in the western theater. Sherman's "total war" campaign as captured by his official photographer. Size: 9 by 12 inches, paperbound.

Price: $7.95.

Catalog of "'Hard-To-Find' 19th Century Military Goods & Reproduction Living History Accessories," $6 within U.S., $10 foreign.

Dixie Leather Works
306 N. 7th Street
Paducah, KY 42001
Phone: 502-442-1058
Fax: 502-442-1049
Order Line: 800-888-5183

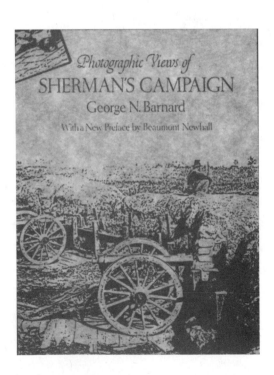

Illustrated Catalog of Civil War Military Goods

An unabridged reprint of the complete 1864 catalog of the Schuyler, Hartley & Graham company. Union weapons, insignia, uniform accessories, and other equipment are included, with pay tables and other incidental information. 160 pages, 9 by 12 inches, paperbound.

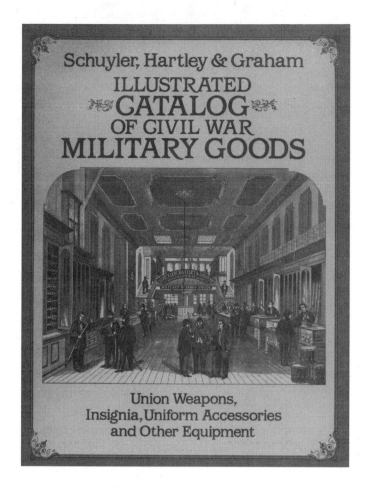

Civil War Etiquette & Dictionary of Vulgarisms

by Martine

First printed in 1866 as *Martine's Handbook of Etiquette*, this 168-page book is "a complete manual for those who desire to understand the rules of good breeding, the customs of good society, and to avoid incorrect and vulgar habits." Included is a reprint of the 1864 *Dictionary of Vulgarisms*.

"General Catalog" available, $2.

Amazon Drygoods
2218 East 11th Street
Davenport, IA 52803-3760
Phone: 319-322-6800
Fax: 319-322-4003
Order Line: 800-798-7979

PERIODICALS

Sanitary Commission Bulletin

This 32-page bulletin reports on the status of all the activities of this predominantly women's commission, formed in June 1861 to give aid to the war's sick and wounded. It contains many sad and inspirational stories and poems accompanied by paid advertisements for life insurance and artificial limbs. An exact reproduction of the original, it measures 5½ by 8½ inches.

U.S. Christian Commission Facts

A practical booklet for those on the home front from this predominantly male commission that served the soldier and tried to improve wartime conditions.

"Soldier, May I Talk To You?"

A religious tract distributed by the U.S. Christian Commission.

Godey's Lady's Book

A reprint of the January 1861 edition of this influential ladies' magazine. It contains fashion plates, patterns, stories, art, and advertising.

Also available is the *Family Medical Almanac* of 1859, and the *Farmer's Almanacs* for the years 1862 through 1864.

General catalog available, $2.

Amazon Drygoods
2218 East 11th Street
Davenport, IA 52803-3760
Phone: 319-322-6800
Fax: 319-322-4003
Order Line: 800-798-7979

Confederate Money

The night they drove old Dixie down, a special "treasure train" was dispatched in pursuit of Jefferson Davis, who had fled Richmond with the government towards the Trans-Mississippi. Carrying $500,000 of the Confederate Treasury's gold and silver, the train caught up with Davis in Abbeville, South Carolina. It was there that the Confederate leader, in consultation with Secretary of War Breckenridge and several brigade commanders, slowly and reluctantly came to accept that, as he put it, "all is indeed lost."

Of the rail-borne treasury money, some $150,000 was paid out to soldiers, and $230,000 sent on to a Georgia bank for deposit. Gold worth $86,000 was concealed in the false bottom of a carriage and started on its way to Charleston for secret shipment to England, where it could be drawn upon if and when the government reached Texas.

Despite this scattering of the bullion that backed it, the twentieth-century admonition to "save your Confederate money" has always been coupled with a hope for Southern resurgence that long survived Davis' Abbeville concession. However, even though the Stars and Bars has never concluded any broadcast days, the saving of Confederate shinplasters has paid off. As Col. Grover Criswell notes in his *Guide to Confederate Money*—an original, uncirculated "Indian Princess" five-dollar Confederate note is now worth 100,000 times its face value.

Today, "The Confederate Treasury" is a Tennessee firm that enjoys an exemplary reputation for its reprinted Confederate money. The "Confederate States Currency 1861-1865" set contains 70 notes, representing all those issued for the Confederate States Treasury Department. The bills, which replicate the look of the originals in precise detail, arrive in a handsome album that can be ordered embossed with its owner's name.

Price: $139.95. Personalized name stamped in gold foil, $10 additional.

The Confederate Treasury Company
1100 North Main Street
Tennessee Ridge, TN 37178
Phone: 615-721-3301
Fax: 615-721-4155
Order Line: 800-632-2383

Stereoscope & Views

Victorian ancestor of virtual reality apparatuses, the stereoscope was the first instrument to exploit the disparity in eyesight that allows an image to be seen three-dimensionally. It was invented in 1837—the year of Victoria's ascent to the throne—a cumbersome box into which viewers were obliged to insert their brilliantined heads. In 1850 a demonstration of a more practicable model stereoscope at London's Crystal Palace Exposition so amused the Queen that the British upper classes immediately took the cue and made stereoscopes the fashion.

An American, Dr. Oliver Wendell Holmes, Sr., developed the more familiar open-frame type in 1859. He turned his pioneering design over to the industry, free of royalties, so that, in the words of Craig Daniels, the stereoscope's current manufacturer, "all the world might sooner and more affordably enjoy stereography (which was exactly what followed)."

Mr. Daniels notes that his pedestal-mounted "SaturnScope" is faithful in both craftsmanship and design to those of the nineteenth century. The instrument can also be handheld.

Price: $160.

Three sets of reproduction views are available: "History, Places, Events," a scattering of views from the turn of the century; "Staged & Posed Subjects"; and a "Sampler Set."

Literature and order form available.

StereoType
P.O. Box 1637
Florence, OR 97439
Phone: 503-997-8879

Dolls

The doll Jack is pardoned by order of the President.

—Abraham Lincoln, in an 1861 pardon written for his son's soldier-doll Jack. The doll had been convicted for the commission of such serious offenses as desertion and sleeping while on duty.

Replicas of the china and porcelain dolls of the period extending from 1850 through 1880 are available.

Catalog, $3.

Antique Doll Reproductions
R.R. 1, Box 103
Milo, MO 64767
Phone: 417-876-4785
417-876-6280 (summers)

"Hopping to the Cat"

Just around 1800, the quadrille, or cotillion was imported from France. As such, it was identifiably the waltz of the Republicans—a Jeffersonian version of the syncopated ball-room-canter held in low regard by Federalists. However, as political passions cooled, even Hamiltonians came around, promenading home to a culture wherein the quadrille joined the reel and contradance as the nightly occupation of everyone from plantation slaves to their fashionable mistresses.

Dancers gathered in homes and taverns, and at raisings, huskings, sleighing parties, and, of course, weddings. Christmas, Thanksgiving, and Election Day occasioned village or plantation balls, "all open and lighted with the best of tallow candles" as Harriet Beecher Stowe recalled their illumination of a New England winter's night. Whether formed into the long lines of rustic contradances or the more sophisticated twin-pairings of the quadrille, these dances provided a setting for communal exultation—a time in which the otherwise overworked and shut-in could gather, commune, and court.

In the 1820s, the "valse"—later waltz—came to America on a Parisian ship. Valsing paired the small group that formed the quadrille into the familiar facing couple that whirled around the ballroom oblivious to the growing religious opposition to dance as an immoral display. However, the revolutions of 1848 aroused much interest in America, and outlandish dances were a way for society to declare its sympathy with European insurgents. By the Civil War, dancing and its reli-gious opposition conducted a two-step of their own, as the former went to and fro in response to the latter's evangelical fervor. Nevertheless, by this time the polka, and such exotic waltz variations as the zingerella, varovienne and koska were also enjoyed.

Combining accurate costuming with period manners, customs, and style, The Commonwealth Vintage Dancers replicate grand balls, dances, and other amusements of the 1850s and 1860s. In addition, they are experienced at teaching classes and leading workshops in the dance styles of this period for beginning through advanced students, endeavors that have earned them the Preservation Award of the New England Chapter of the Victorian Society of America.

The Commonwealth Vintage Dancers organize, perform, and instruct the dances of the late nineteenth century (the 1890s) and the Ragtime era (1900 through the 1920s) with the same allegiance to period etiquette and costume. Every summer, their company hosts the Holiday of Vintage Dance, "a week-long extravaganza of dance and amusements in and around the mansions of Newport, Rhode Island."

Brochure available.

The Commonwealth Vintage Dancers
99 Malvern Street
Melrose, MA 02176
Phone: 617-396-2870

Jefferson Davis

Jefferson Finis Davis was the Confederacy's first and only president—a succinct résumé containing much in the way of isolation, tragedy, and greatness.

An 1828 graduate of West Point, Davis left the army after serving in the Northwest frontier. After eloping with Zachary Taylor's beautiful daughter, Sarah Knox Taylor, in 1835, he settled down to a semi-obscure life as a Mississippi planter. His first wife having died three months into their marriage,

Davis married again, to Varina Howell, and ran for the U.S. Congress. In 1846 he resigned his seat to serve in the Mexican War, receiving a severe wound at the battle of Buena Vista. After returning to public life, Davis was made Secretary of War by Franklin Pierce in 1853. In 1861 he was chosen provisional president of the Confederacy in a compromise between moderates and extremists, and was inaugurated as president of the permanent government on February 22, 1862. Any actor intent on portraying Davis would do well to emulate the picture painted by cabinet member Judah Benjamin, Steven Vincent Benét's epic poem, *John Brown's Body*:

… you are the South in word,
Deed, thought and temper, the cut cameo
Brittle but durable, refined but fine…
The mind set in tradition, but not unjust,
The generous slaveholder, the gentleman
Who neither forces his gentility
Nor lets it be held lightly—

Unlike Lincoln, Davis' Civil War didn't end with his life, but both men gave their lives over to the war without reservation. There was never any question that, despite the loss of beloved children, both had to endure. In the face of sickliness and an increasingly attenuated appearance, the Southern president was his Northern counterpart's equal in resilience. And whereas Lincoln's homeliness betrayed a warrior's humanity, Davis' taut look was honest packaging for the steadfastness within.

Your eyes look tired.
Your face looks more and more like John Calhoun.
And that is just, because you are his son
In everything but blood, the austere child
Of his ideas, the flower of states-rights.

Although he was described by one biographer as having an imperious temper, Davis' "gift of warming men"—while no match for Lincoln's gentle good nature—helped bring the Confederacy within a holler of independence. Davis publicly regretted Lincoln's death, while Lincoln, easing himself into

Davis' abandoned chair in Richmond, went mute after asking for a glass of water. Both were native Kentuckians, born within a year of each other. As presidents, they were separated by no more than 30 leagues—two supreme commanders haunting the charred territory of cause and country. "We are not fighting for slavery," Davis once said, "we are fighting for independence, and that—or extermination—we will have." The defeated Davis survived the South's war for independence, while—in a wrenching irony of history—it was the victorious Lincoln whom the war exterminated.

New Yorker Peter Blaisdell's career as Jefferson Davis began on the evening in 1981 that he attended a Blue and Gray Ball hosted by a local Confederate unit of reenactors. As he entered the ballroom, he was astonished to see troops there bring themselves to attention and salute. His surprise turned to bafflement the moment the unit's colonel approached to salute smartly, deliver a detailed report, salute again, and withdraw.

The colonel returned to apologize, stating his hope that he had not embarrassed Mr. Blaisdell. "Are you aware," he asked his extravagantly welcomed guest "that you look just like Jefferson Davis?" The colonel explained that while there was at least one "Lincoln" at most Civil War events, no Jeff Davis ever appeared, and that Confederate reenactors needed a president of their own.

Thus began an odyssey that started with Blaisdell's desire to credibly and intelligently perform as Davis and ended with the actor's conviction in the rightness of the Southern cause. In debates with Jim Getty's Lincoln, Mr. Blaisdell has been called upon to defend this position at the Civil War Society's conventions.

Over the past fifteen years, Blaisdell has appeared before numerous other groups, including the National Park Service, the Smithsonian Institution, and Civil War Roundtables from New York to Houston. He is best known for "The Other Side of Gettysburg," in which Southern grievances against the North are made in a point-by-point response to the Gettysburg Address. A member of the Sons of Confederate Veterans, Mr. Blaisdell has written, codirected, and appeared

in "Southside Shadows," a one-act play recreating the meeting of the Confederate cabinet on April 8, 1865—the eve of Lee's surrender.

Peter Blaisdell
P.O. Box 725
Naples, NY 14512
Phone: 716-374-9282

Abraham Lincoln

Wherever Abraham Lincoln is today, we wonder how he feels about actors. In a speech made just prior to his assassination, Lincoln acknowledged Lee's defeat with an entreaty that charity rather than malice be shown to all. Soon after, a nation of mourners could not resist bestowing upon this doleful and forgiving man—this martyr who had only just delivered the Union—the secular image of a Federal Christ.

Still, we are discussing *actors* here.

Raymond Massey, Henry Fonda, and Charles Middleton (better remembered as "Ming the Merciless" in the old Flash Gordon serials) tried, with varying degrees of failure, to portray the Great Emancipator. Perhaps even Olivier, Reagan, and all the Booths would make high school productions of their efforts capture the sixteenth president's enormous complexity. For in addition to the familiarly honest, homespun, emancipating Abe there is Lincoln the henpecked; Lincoln the seer; Lincoln the sentimentalist; and Lincoln tormented by sons lost in addition to his own. Add to this the lesser-known Lincolns that scholars are bringing to light: the tongue-tied politician; the physically powerful athlete; the deceptively able forebear of modern, internationalist presidents; and the citizen-general whose military acumen was wars ahead of the West Point generation he commanded. Finally, there is Lincoln the Twain, Lincoln the Churchill and—as alluded to above—Lincoln the national saviour.

While it may be easier imagining Lincoln's forgiveness of Booth than of, say, Jane Fonda—just think of what the President's regard must be for those whose portrayals of him are nearly inseparable from tribute. Certainly Henry Fonda falls into this category, as do others whose reward is far smaller and devotion perhaps greater.

Jim Getty has been involved in productions since his high school years. He holds a Master of Music degree from Illinois Wesleyan University, and was director of choral activities at the University of Maine. Having created his monologue, "Mr. Lincoln Returns to Gettysburg," Mr. Getty and his wife Joanne moved there themselves in 1977. Ever since, he has reprised the role during each season while maintaining a national schedule of Lincoln presentations for schools, colleges, conventions, and other events. In keeping with these, Mr. Getty has portrayed Lincoln for the Library of Congress and the Smithsonian Institution, and his presentations involving the interaction of participants have been part of managerial workshops for MCI, the Tigrett Corporation's "Lessons from Lincoln," and the Graduate School of Retail Bank Management of the University of Virginia. Finally, Mr. Getty offers Lincoln programs for the Delta Queen Steamboat Company on their Civil War cruises each year.

Brochure available.

A. Lincoln's Place
460 Baltimore Street
Gettysburg, PA 17325
Phone: 717-334-6049

Portraits of Military & Historic Figures

In an 1871 print entitled "Lost Cause," a Confederate battle flag looms like a divine specter above a soldier's melancholy homecoming. In the postwar South, the cessation of hostilities brought with it more than the loss of a war—it brought the defeat of a country and the cause that fostered its attempt at independence. To soften their injury, Southern whites elevated such emblems as the battle flag to the status of sacred relics. During Reconstruction, when the South was occupied by Northern armies, this Lost Cause legend rationalized the defeat as one to an inferior, but nonetheless overpowering, oppressor. As one century ended and another began, the movement exalted Dixie's memory by idealizing its conduct in "The War of Northern Aggression," by sentimentalizing its antebellum institutions, and by sanctifying Southern symbols in poetry, books, and painting.

While many Yankee personages are included, the military and historic figure paintings offered by Classic Portraits are evidence of the fact that a kind of Lost Cause sentiment—one expanded to recognize the shared experience of both sides—remains with us. As if cognizant of this, the company's oil paintings aren't reproduced by means of some clever transfer process, but rather are individual works painted by artists on staff.

Classic Portraits' canvasses are available from a rotating inventory of subjects. As of this writing these include: Robert E. Lee, Joshua Chamberlain, Nathan B. Forrest, Abraham Lincoln, John S. Mosby, Stonewall Jackson, Jefferson Davis, George A. Custer, James Longstreet, William T. Sherman, Sitting Bull, George Washington, and J.E.B. Stuart (shown at right).

Dimensions: 20 by 24 inches.

Custom-painted canvasses of ancestors, scenes, historic figures, and other subjects can also be hand-painted from your color or black-and-white photographs.

Prices: Unframed stock oil paintings, $150 to $265, depending on the artist, subject, and approximate appraisal value.

Free brochure obtainable.

Classic Portraits Fine Arts
4 Marshs Victory Court
Baltimore, MD 21228
Phone: 410-747-8780
For orders and reports
on current inventory: 800-677-3257

CAMPGROUND

"Even when one adds the small engagements to the big battles he does not tell the whole story of war. Much of every soldier's life was sheer boredom—killing time in camp when the rains turned the roads into impassable morasses."

—Paul M. Angle
The Civil War Years

TENTS

For Civil War soldiers the moonlit portals of a tent could be as gateways to a fearsome and exciting adventure. As a New Englander recalled: "one cannot describe his feelings during the first night under a tent—the beginning of his real soldier life. There was so much to look forward to, so much to look back upon. Thoughts of separation from home and loved ones, never, perhaps, to be seen again. All the hopes and ambitions of the young soldier were crowding through the brain, ending in the one dearest wish to go speedily to the front." By 1864 when Walter Kittredge's "Tenting on the Old Camp Ground" became popular, this soldier was odds-on less enthusiastic about the front and more inclined towards the song's sentiment that, whilst tenting, "Many are the hearts that are weary tonight, wishing for the war to cease."

Sibley Tent

Inspired by the tipi, the conical tent designed before the war by Henry Hopkins Sibley is the conflict's most recognizable field shelter. The tent measured 12 feet in height and 18 feet in diameter, "large enough for a good size circus side show," as another New Englander said. Although made to sleep twelve men arrayed as wheel spokes (at the hub of which could be a fire), the tent was generally inhabited by fifteen or twenty, each using his knapsack to mark his territory. The soldiers would deliver themselves into the arms of Morpheus as a suffering circle of spoons, and—according to the aforementioned Yankee—"if one wanted to turn over to give the bones on the other side a chance, he would yell out the order to 'flop' and all would go together…".

The Sibley tent proved too cumbersome to transport for use in the field, and passed out of use in 1862. By that time its maker was a Confederate Brigadier, commanding the Department of New Mexico.

Panther Primitives' Sibley tents are made "just like the original." The front opening is "an authentic 8' 9" tall," while the rear ventilation doorway is 5 feet high. The base of the tent is secured with reinforced brass spur washer grommets, which are set through four layers of canvas.

Prices From $270 to $470, depending on the type of treated, 100-percent cotton-duck canvas selected.

Wedge Tent

Everyone is crying, Everyone is cross.

—From the 1862 letter of a New York soldier stationed in Virginia, describing conditions in his wedge tent.

The intended replacement for the Sibley dormitory was a tent six feet square (sometimes seven feet wide) set upon a ridge pole less than five feet above the ground. Also referred to as "A" tents, the wedges could accommodate four to six men in progressive levels of discomfort—each either prone, recumbent, or stooped. Panther has wedge tents available in several sizes.

Wall & Hospital Tents

Relatively luxurious wall tents were distinguished by the fact that they had four upright sides, and some even had walk-in doors. While the Army of the Potomac was on the Virginia Peninsula, McClellan issued a general order prescribing wall tents for general, field, and staff officers, while each line officer was granted a shelter tent of his own.

Panther's wall tents come with standard rolled canvas peg loops, spur washer brass grommets, and overlapping flaps on the door end. They make their tents in the two sizes that were most common: The Type 1, measuring 10 feet 6 inches wide by 11 feet 6 inches long by 7 feet high, with 45 inch walls; and the Type 2, measuring 8 feet 9 inches square by 8 feet 6 inches high, with 45 inch walls.

The wall tent was often used in the field as a hospital tent. These mid-1800s MASHs came in many sizes, with some accommodating up to twenty patients. Sometimes two tents would be joined in such a way as to allow for a central corridor to run the double-tent's entire length. On either side of this passage would stand a double row of cots for the wounded and infirm.

Panther's Civil War hospital tent measures 14 feet in width by 14 feet 2 inches in length. It has 45-inch-high walls and a variety of tent-fly arrangements.

Half-Shelter ("Dog" or "Pup") Tent

We have to draw purp tents as we call them. They are little tents big enough for too.

— LaForest Dunham of the 129th Illinois.

The half-shelters were so named because each man carrying a piece of the tent was given instructions to seek out another so equipped, whereupon they would have pieces enough to button together a tent of somewhat-waterproof canvas. That was in 1862. By '64, the tent's dimensions were enlarged, and a third "half" (carried by a third soldier) became available as an end piece. These *tentes d'Chien* were patterned after the French *tentes d'Abri* and 300,000 were issued to Federal forces the year that the Sibleys were retired. Some soldiers hated the contortions required by this trade-off, as one Massachusetts trooper complained: "to enter one of these 'dog kennels' ... you had to get down on your knees, with your head near the earth, as though you were approaching the throne of an Arabian monarch, and crawl in."

Catalog of Early American frontier replicas, $2.

Panther Primitives
P.O. Box 32
Normantown, WV 25267
Phone: 304-462-7718
Order Line: 800-487-2684

Similar replicas available from:

Red Willow Clothing and Canvas Shelters
Box 188
131 West Main Street
Oxford, IA 52322
Phone: 319-628-4815

BLANKETS

But now, there they go, one by one; no, two by two. Down goes an old rubber blanket, and then a good, thick, woolen one, probably with a big 'U.S.' in the centre of it. Down go two men. They are hidden under another of the 'U.S.' blankets ... They love each other to the death, those men, and sleep there, like little children, locked in close embrace.

—Carlton McCarthy, Pvt., 2nd Company Richmond Howitzers, in his book, *Detailed Minutiae of Soldier Life in the Army of Northern Virginia, 1861-1865*, 1882.

Rarely are soldierly accounts written with the lyricism of McCarthy's memoir, and we are fortunate for their details, which afford epigraphs as revealing as the above. Rare too— and poetic—is the devotion to detail found in the Civil War-era replicas produced by Paris, Ohio's County Cloth. These works are certainly no less revealing—and afford all the experience of the minutiae of the Civil War soldier's existence.

Model 1851 Army Standard Blanket

This gray blanket was used throughout the Civil War. Its center design, a three-line "U.S." legend hand-embroidered with yarn, distinguishes it as a replica of the war's most frequently encountered blanket. County Cloth's Army Standard blanket is made of 100 percent wool, that has been spun, twisted, and dyed to precisely match the originals. (The two such blankets extant are both in the possession of the Danish government, which received them in the 1850s as part of an international exchange of military equipment.) The blankets measure 68 by 84 inches.

Two other versions of this blanket, one bearing a serif- and the other a block-lettered U.S. legend, have been documented from existing examples. These are available from County Cloth upon request.

Price: $156.

Price list for military blankets, fabrics, and garment kits available with swatch card, $5.

County Cloth
13797-C Georgetown Street, S.E.
Paris, OH 44669
Phone: 330-862-3307
Fax: 330-862-3304

"Auggie Weissert's Blanket," another exhaustively researched U.S. blanket replica, available from:

Wisconsin Veterans Museum
30 W. Mifflin Street
Madison, WI 53703
Phone: 608-266-1680

Hudson's Bay Point Blankets

If we do strike at them Yankees again, they will get one of the worst whippings they ever had for most of the boys are mighty anxious to get a lick at them for some blankets.

-Pvt. William H. Cody, in a letter to his sister.

It was by such means that most Confederates were able to secure the U.S. Model 1851 blankets described opposite. Other blankets used by the Southern army were often brought from home and included the Hudson's Bay blankets introduced into American trade in 1779. Loomed in England of 100 percent pure virgin wool, these blankets are available today in four sizes: four point (regular), six point (queen) and eight point (king).

Available colors and patterns are: scarlet, gold, green, white, white with blue stripe, white with gold stripe, and candy-stripe. The eight-point blankets are available in candy-stripe only.

For dealer information contact:

Woolrich Inc.
Woolrich, PA 17779
Phone: 717-769-6464
Fax: 717-769-6470
Order Line: 800-995-1299

Gen. U.S. Grant strikes a pose alongside his folding camp chair.

Camp Tables & Chairs

"Beyond the fame they acquired from being photographed in every theater of the war," writes Stephen Alexander of Second Empire Fine Furniture, "the thing that most attracted me to reproducing these pieces was their beauty and characteristic Victorian ingenuity." Seemingly, no crass market forces can undermine the importance Mr. Alexander places on the uniqueness and intrinsic beauty of the artifacts he replicates. His camp table and chairs, which constitute three-fourths of a carefully cultivated Civil War line (there is also a telescope tripod, described in the Field chapter), "have a grace and elegance not uncommon to military design of the period."

To accompany his folding oak camp table, Alexander researched "museums, collectors, and suppliers" for his first camp chair, which has bentwood oak arms and back slats, and an upholstered seat made with a Persian rug

edged in wool binding. An armless oaken folding camp chair is also available.

Dimensions, which may be altered to suit customer, are: Table open, 26 inches high by 20 inches long by 15 inches wide; closed, 33 inches long by 9 inches wide. Armchair open, 34 inches high with a seat 19 inches wide by 15 inches deep; closed, 24 inches long by 21 inches wide by 9 inches high. Armless chair open, 32 inches high with a seat 22 inches wide by 16 inches deep; closed, 32 inches long by 9 inches high.

Prices: Camp table, $175; armless folding chair, $200; armchair, $350.

Second Empire Fine Furniture
2927 Guilford Avenue
Baltimore, MD 21218
Phone: 410-366-7244

Camp Mirrors

The anthropologist Desmond Morris said that in certain cultures it became possible for males "to make a statement of allegiance or rebellion" by aping or defying a ruler's growth of beard. This was difficult during the Civil War, when not only presidents and generals, but just about everyone on either side from long-haired radical to mossbacked Whig sported the chin-whiskers to match. Still, the Civil War's many sideburns and Vandykes require tending, and for those (as well as for

extended periods of somber reflection) a camp mirror is available. Replicas of camp-style hanging mirrors are available.

Catalog of "Civil War Era Items," 75¢.

Kentwood Sutlery and Manufacturing
P.O. Box 88201
Kentwood, MI 49518
Phone: 616-531-7645

Hardware & Equipment

Kentucky Axe

In his book, *The Civil War Collector's Encyclopedia*, Francis A. Lord notes that the numbers of axes found on Civil War battlefields and at campsites testify to the reliance that both armies placed on the tool, and its similarity to modern-day counterparts.

As described by Mr. Charles Keller of Forge & Anvil, the Kentucky axe actually dates to the eighteenth century, when it was set to the task of clearing eastern woodland for homesteads. Mr. Keller—who researches the history of the tools he makes as thoroughly as he does their design—confirms that the Kentucky axe was routinely used by both sides during the Civil War to construct fortifications and camps, as well as to cut firewood.

Forge & Anvil's Kentucky axes are produced according to techniques developed during the 1840s and were still in use twenty years hence. Their cutting edges are made of high-carbon steel that is fitted between two pieces of softer iron, with the whole welded together under a trip-hammer. The handles are crafted from seasoned ash that is worked with draw knife, rasp, and scraper before being rubbed with oil. After a final grinding, the axes are given a finish of asphaltum varnish in the nineteenth-century manner.

Price: $165.

Catalog of nineteenth century-style tools available.

Forge & Anvil
P.O Box 51
Newman, IL 61942
Phone: 217-352-0803

Barrels & Kegs

Aside from their obvious utility as containers for foodstuffs and supplies, Union troops employed barrels as a disciplinary tool. Army tradition held that thieving, insubordinate, or drunk soldiers were to be paraded around the compound under armed guard. The offending soldier would be naked, save for an outer garment of barrel.

Panther Primitives' barrels and kegs are made of solid white oak and lined with paraffin. They are available in sizes capable of containing 5, 10, and 15 gallons.

Catalog of Early American frontier replicas, $2.

Panther Primitives
P.O. Box 32
Normantown, WV 25267
Phone: 304-462-7718
Order Line: 800-487-2684

Laundry Tub

Making war was strictly white-collar work for Union Maj. Gen. Winfield Scott Hancock. Although his shirts were standard issue, his aides reported that if blood or gunpowder soiled one in battle, the general would momentarily retire to his tent and don a fresh replacement.

A replica of the kind of double-handled laundry tub that must have attained special status in Hancock's camp is available.

Dimensions: Bottom diameter, 18 inches; top, 24 inches; depth 12 inches. Available by special order only.

Price: $65.

Camp Pail

Similar to those of the period, this pail has a 2 gallon capacity.

Price: $26.

Pitcher and basin also obtainable.

Catalog specializing in period tinware available.

The Village Tinsmithing Works
P.O. Box 189
Randolph, OH 44265
Phone: 330-325-9101

Wooden Buckets

Intended as containers for butter or lard, "firkins" were often used to hold water, nails, and other supplies useful in camp.

Panther Primitives' wooden buckets are paraffin-lined and have rope handles. They have an approximate three-quarter gallon capacity.

Price: $24

Catalog of Early American frontier items, $2.

Panther Primitives
P.O. Box 32
Normantown, WV 25267
Phone: 304-462-7718
Order Line: 800-487-2684

Hardtack

Two syllables, well chosen. The standard bread of the Federal armies was three-and-a-half-square inches of baked flour, water, and salt that was distributed to soldiers in one-pound lots. Hard as Harvard Law, these "teeth dullers" could not be eaten unless first soaked—and nothing could keep them from setting up shop as a Willard's Hotel for grubs.

You may now buy the replica, but the hardtack that at least one Pennsylvanian got in 1861 was a collectible. Believing the camp gossip, he claimed the crackers he'd been issued had been "in storage since the Mexican War," while another soldier said that his biscuits' résumés included service as ordnance with Perry in Japan. Still even this hardtack must have seemed bakery-fresh to those troops who, after opening crates of the bread labeled "B.C." (for brigade commissary) assumed the initials indicated a date of manufacture. Wags also found the hardtack-as-ammo simile difficult to resist, as when an Illinois private recommended it as the stuff with which to "load our guns" and kill "sesechs in a hurry" in what might have been the only action in the Food Fight Between the States.

On the march, a piece of hardtack was often removed from the haversack and placed in the cheek where it was marinated to a safe consistency with saliva. Here the bread's high sodium content made it useful as a kind of salt tablet. The salt also made hardtack mouse- and roach-proof, a matter as important to the weevils who took up residence in these "worm castles" as it was to the soldiers who carried them. After all, worms and maggots not only ate less of the ration than mice, they fortified it with an (admittedly repulsive) form of protein.

However, even infested crackers "ate better than they looked," according to one New Englander with a sheet-iron stomach. Of course, he soaked his in coffee first. You may want to try other recipes:

Skillygalee

Take hardtack. Fry in bacon grease. Soak in water. Serve.

Hellfire Stew

Take hardtack. Crush with rock or rifle butt. Repeat three final directions above.

Lobcourse

Make a soup of hardtack, salt pork, and whatever else is available. Serve.

Bully Soup, or Panada

Take hardtack, pound with rock or rifle butt. Mix with cornmeal, wine and ginger. Stir. Heat. Serve.

Finally, hardtack is holy communion for Civil War buffs. And—if it doesn't leave you gumming verses of "We are Coming, Father Abraham" just like Gabby Hayes—it'll grow on you.

The Mechanical Baking Company offers hardtack in allotments of 1-100 biscuits. It considers its U.S. government specification hardtack cracker a "valid replica of the biscuit used during the mid-1800s."

Price list available.

Mechanical Baking Company
P.O. Box 513
Pekin, Illinois 61555-0513
Phone: 309-353-2414

Ham & Bacon

"Black as a shoe" on the outside, Civil War meat rations were usually also "yellow with putrefaction" within. Sowbelly, the soldier's term for pork, was usually in short supply—although one Rhode Islander complained that he and his fellows had received so much they were "inclined to speak in grunts, prick up [their] ears, and perform other animal demonstrations."

In 1864, one of Confederate Gen. John Bell Hood's hungry Texans remarked that if he was ever so fortunate as to return to his father's house he would "take a hundred biscuit and two large hams … and eat it all at one meal." The Cumberland General Store's old-fashioned smoked ham and slab bacon more closely resembles this, the stuff of Civil War soldiers' dreams. Both are dry cured slowly, according to nineteenth-century methods.

Prices: Country ham, 13 to 15 pounds, $48; country slab bacon, 15 pounds, $31.

Catalog of "Goods in Endless Variety for Man and Beast," $4.

Cumberland General Store
#1 Highway 68
Crossville, TN 38555
Order line: 800-334-4640
Fax: 615-456-1211

Corn Meal

Not to be outdone, Confederates generally quartered their worms in corn bread made from coarse, unsifted meal. When the raw meal was issued, soldiers often preferred to fry out some bacon until the pan was half-filled with grease, then mix the meal with water "until it flows like milk." Poured into the skillet and cooked, the resulting dirty-brown mixture was called "slosh" or "coosh."

By contrast, Indian Head stone-ground corn meal is an excellently refined flour. Its bag, however, has the sachem-in-profile aspect of a nineteenth-century product. Available in white or yellow corn meal.

Recipe booklet, $1 with "Washington" trademark from package.

Wilkins-Rogers, Inc.
P.O. Box 308
Ellicott City, MD 21041
Phone: 410-465-5800

FRUITS & VEGETABLES

Vegetables were hard to come by in field and camp, where the want of them often caused scurvy. The Federal Army countered with dehydrated cakes of compacted turnips, carrots, onions, beets, beans, and other vegetables. These the quartermaster referred to as "desiccated and compressed mixed vegetables," but to the men who contended with their dry tangle of roots, leaves, tops, and stalks they were simply "baled hay." Among Confederates, Stonewall Jackson's fondness for lemons (he frequently sucked them, even in battle) kept scurvy at bay, but foot soldiers were advised by their commissaries to forage for wild onions.

The Landis Valley Museum's "Heirloom Seed Catalog" is an expression of its Heirloom Seed Project's "central purpose … to encourage the preservation of traditional strains of historic open-pollinated varieties of plant material … which have an oral or written history extending back into the early 1800s."

Winnigstadt Cabbage

Described in the Landis Valley catalog as "an old favorite from the 1860s," this is a German cabbage with firm, pointed heads and yellowish-green leaves.

Price: $2.50 per packet of seeds.

Jenny Lind Melon

Jenny Lind, and Burr's New Pine, are good early fruits.

— From an 1861 patent report.

While today no bodegas display the Madonna ribbed cuke, seeds for the green-fleshed melons named for the popular nineteenth-century diva, Jenny Lind, are available. These result in fruit weighing between one and two pounds. Unfortunately, the seeds are in short supply and must be ordered early in the year.

Price: $2.50 per packet of seeds.

Golden Russet Apples

This fruit dates to 1845, at least. The apples are medium-sized, roundish, and colored a golden russet with bronze cheeks. The yellowish flesh is described as being moderately crisp, juicy, and carrying a "nearly apricot-like aromatic flavor."

Price: $2 per scion (stick).

Heirloom seed catalog available, $4 (in Canada, $5).

Landis Valley Museum
Heirloom Seed Project
2451 Kissel Hill Road
Lancaster, PA 17601
Phone: 717-569-0401

Similar items obtainable from:

Seed Savers Exchange
3076 North Winn Road
Decorah, IA 52101
Phone & Fax: 319-382-5872

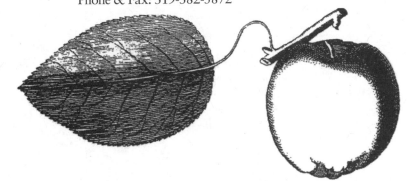

Sarsaparilla

On the outside ... is printed the following thirsty announcement ... Congress Water, Sarsaparilla Soda, Ginger Champaign [etc.].

—Uncle Sam, pseud., *Peculiarities*, 1844.

Termed the "Soda-Water Bottle" because of its shape, the Dahlgren gun helped bottle up southern ports under the watchful eyes of its creator, Union Adm. John A. Dahlgren, commander of the South Atlantic Blockading Squadron.

Actual, "authentic-like" (and far more conventional) soda bottles contain sarsaparilla, a more popular drink during the Civil War than today.

Price: $18 per case.

Catalog of "Civil War Era Items," 75¢.

Kentwood Sutlery and Manufacturing
P.O. Box 88201
Kentwood, MI 49518
Phone: 616-531-7645

Food Tin Labels

Were one to travel into the past, two marvels would continually present themselves: the first, consisting of all that is astonishingly unfamiliar; and the second, made up of all that is astonishingly familiar. Return to the Civil War and you may take your pick of unfamiliar things: slavery, honor, seaboard wilderness, cheap seafood, and fainting women. For a familiar experience, just wander into camp and lighten your instant coffee with some Borden's Condensed Milk.

Replica Civil War food tin labels for sardines, peaches, raisins, Distelfink Canneries Beans, Soldier's Joy Army Beans & Bacon Soup and other camp delicacies are available sans tins.

Price: 25¢ to $1.75 each.

Free price list of cartridges, ammunition boxes, labels, and souvenirs obtainable.

Cartridges Unlimited
4320-A Hartford Street
St. Louis, MO 63116
Phone: 314-664-4332

The Irish Brigade

The Irish Brigade is remembered for distinguishing itself at the devastating assault on Marye's Heights during the Fredericksburg campaign.

In November of 1862, General Ambrose Everett Burnside, after replacing George McClellan as Commander of the Army of the Potomac, exhibited enough of his predecessor's wariness to both encourage Lee and further depress Lincoln. Having advanced cautiously south toward the Rappahannock, the new chief was in a position to strike between the wings of Lee's army, defeating them in detail. Using a tactic reminiscent of McClellan, Burnside forsook this advantage, preferring instead to encamp above the icy river and await the arrival of a pontoon bridge with which to cross it. However, the bridge was caught in the snail's pace of Federal supply and didn't arrive until the 25th, by which time Lee had secured an excellent defensive position in the hills on the right bank. From this ground, Lee awaited Burnside with a reunited army of 78,000.

Gen. Burnside finally moved to cross the Rappahannock on December 11, but his tardy and confusing orders helped bring Gen. Edwin Sumner's men, who were traversing the river opposite Marye's Heights (at the high, north end of the ridge behind Fredericksburg) under severe fire from rebel sharpshooters stationed in the town. After launching a splintering but unsuccessful bombardment to dislodge these, Union infantry crossed the Rappahannock in boats and built the bridge. This allowed troops that included the Irish Brigade to mass at the base of Marye's Heights on December 13, undertaking a series of futile but determined assaults at which modern commanders marvel. As one veteran recalled, the blue-backs advanced through rebel volleys as if "breasting a storm of rain and sleet, their faces and bodies being only half-turned to [it], with their shoulders shrugged." In this way, the Heights' defenders under the command of Gen. James Longstreet created a lesser height of Federal dead at its base. By day's end, five major assaults on Marye's Heights were all repulsed by Longstreet, who swore to Lee that he could defeat the entire Yankee nation were it to attack him thus. General Lee, who had earlier commented that it was well that war is so terrible "lest we grow too fond of it," seemed wistful at battle's end: "I wish these people would go away," he said, "and leave us alone."

Seed Potatoes

I will not move my army without onions.

— Ulysses S. Grant

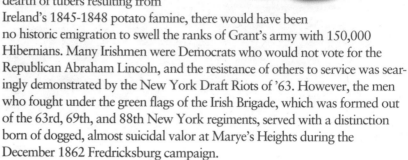

The same could be said for potatoes. In fact, were it not for the dearth of tubers resulting from Ireland's 1845-1848 potato famine, there would have been no historic emigration to swell the ranks of Grant's army with 150,000 Hibernians. Many Irishmen were Democrats who would not vote for the Republican Abraham Lincoln, and the resistance of others to service was searingly demonstrated by the New York Draft Riots of '63. However, the men who fought under the green flags of the Irish Brigade, which was formed out of the 63rd, 69th, and 88th New York regiments, served with a distinction born of dogged, almost suicidal valor at Marye's Heights during the December 1862 Fredricksburg campaign.

Described by one contemporary account as resembling "a dirty brook with leaves floating around," desiccated potatoes was a dish served to Union troops in the wayward belief that it prevented scurvy. Relative to the shooting ability of its defenders, scurvy was not the worst problem at Marye's Heights. Nevertheless, for the preparation of this Civil War delicacy (or any other involving potatoes), we recommend Early Roses—an 1861 variety of seed potato that is still available. Described as having "light pink skin with deep-set eyes and white flesh," the Early Rose of Idaho sounds as worthy of a ballad as the yellow variety of Texas. The seed potatoes are claimed by their growers to propagate vigorously, "yielding large amounts of long tubers."

Prices: Early roses are limited to a 2½ lb. package for $6.75 postpaid, and a 1½ lb. package for $4.25 postpaid.

Catalog $1 to readers of this book.

Ronniger's Potatoes
Star Route
Moyie Springs, Idaho 83845
Phone: 208-267-793
Fax: 208-267-3265

Camp Potatoes

Cut the vegetable into thin slices and throw them into cold water for half an hour; the put them into fat hissing hot, and fry them until they acquire a golden hue. Some persons cut them only into quarters, but they are not near so crisp and nice.

— From *Camp Fires and Camp Cooking or Culinary Hints for the Soldier* by Capt. James M. Sanderson, Commissary of Subsistence of Volunteers, U.S. Government Printing Office, 1862.

Tabasco® Pepper Sauce

As if geologically destined for historic importance, Avery Island rises out of Louisiana's coastal swamp, some 152 feet of rock-salt covered by eons of alluvial sediment. After the war began, John Marsh Avery, scion of the family that owned the island, discovered the salt deposit while working its brine springs to supply the Confederate army. This made the place a military tar-get, and in April 1863, Union troops under the command of Gen. Nathan P. Banks advanced from New Orleans to destroy its salt mines. Judge D.D. Avery and his family were forced to flee into Texas.

Avery Island Saltworks During Reconstruction.

In the summer of 1865, the war over, the Averys returned to the island. Although everything there appeared to have been destroyed, in the midst of the judge's trampled kitchen garden one plant flourished, a South American capsicum (chili) pepper that had taken root there only a decade earlier. Gazing down on their chili, it must've been as if the Averys saw a botanical Scarlett O'Hara telling them that—despite the state of their Gulf Coast Tara—they would never go hungry again.

Edmund McIlhenny, the judge's son-in-law and a gourmet, was taken with the piquant flavor of the peppers and began to experiment with them—first crushing and straining them into a mash with Avery Island salt, and slowly aging the mixture in wooden barrels. The mash was later mixed with strong vinegar, and the seeds removed. The hot sauce he developed lent some zip to the plain fare of Reconstruction, and by 1868, Mr. McIlhenny was selling hundreds of the two-ounce bottles of what he trademarked as Tabasco brand pepper sauce.

Within one year the sauce received its patent, and by 1872 McIlhenny had to open a London office to handle the European demand. Today, the hot sauce from the plant that stood up to Federal occupation still defies the competition.

Recipe booklet and Tabasco® Country Store catalog available.

McIlhenny Company
Avery Island, LA 70513
Phone: 800-634-9599

Reconstruction Hopping John

The greatest luxury with which [the slaves] are acquainted is a stew of bacon and peas, with red pepper, which they call "Hopping John."

— *Frederick Law Olmsted,* A Journey in the Seaboard Slave States, 1861.

Not that Hopping John was solely the provender of slaves. In her 1838 book, Recollections of a Southern Matron, *Caroline Gilman remembered the dish as the greatest of the delicacies that her "papa" brought to the big house table. Still, the scarcity imposed on the South by war and Recon-struction made pea- and bean-based meals such as Hopping John household staples at all levels of society. The stew, which is also traditionally eaten for good fortune on New Year's Day, bene-fits from a liberal dowsing with hot sauce. This 1868 recipe comes from the McIlhenny company.*

1 lb. dried black-eyed peas
3 pints cold water
1/2 lb. sliced salt pork or bacon
1 tsp. Tabasco sauce
1/2 tsp. salt
2 Tbs. bacon fat or lard
2 medium onions, chopped
1 cup uncooked long-grain rice
1 1/2 cups boiling water

Cover the peas with cold water in a large kettle. Soak overnight (the modern method for cooking dried peas involves bringing them to a boil, simmering them for two minutes, and letting them stand for an hour). Add salt pork, Tabasco sauce, and salt. Cover and cook over low heat about 30 minutes. Meanwhile, cook onions in bacon fat until yellow, then add to peas along with rice and boiling water. Cook this mixture until rice is tender and water is absorbed, about 20 to 25 minutes, stirring occa-sionally. Yield: about eight servings.

Bill Hoover, the "Village Tinsmith" of Randolph, Ohio, fashions his tinware from early- to mid-1800s tinsmithing machines and "old-style" hand tools and stakes. The tinware replicates Civil War military-issue and photo-documented non-issue items which have come into Mr. Hoover's possession as owned, borrowed, or museum-loaned artifacts. These artifacts may have included the soldier's personal mess kit that consisted of his tin dipper or cup, tin plate, knife, fork, and spoon. However, camp mess equipment also comprised larger and more cumbersome cooking utensils.

Large Cook Pot

"Similar to those of the period," with a lid and bail. Dimensions: 11½ inches high by 11 inches in diameter.

Price: $60.

Skillet

Made of heavy-duty sheet steel with a riveted handle. Called "creepers" by some Massachusetts men, skillets were usually made of thin wrought iron according to Lord's *Encyclopedia*. Dimensions: 9-inch-diameter by 2 inches deep.

Price: $18.

Catalog specializing in period tinware available.

The Village Tinsmithing Works
P.O. Box 189
Randolph, OH 44265
Phone: 330-325-9101

Military Cup & Bail

Follows military specifications of 1858. Made with heavy-weight tin measuring 4 inches by 4 inches. Wired rim and handle, the latter riveted with lead-free solder.

Price: $15.50.

Tin Plate

Measured from an artifact in the collection of the Quartermaster Museum at Fort Lee, in Petersburg, Virginia. Often improvised as a skillet.

Price: $16.50.

Large Coffeepot

"Coffee was the main stay," recalled a volunteer from the 10th Massachusetts, "without it was misery." Indeed, Army officials were determined that coffee would be the last foodstuff that soldiers would lack. A.C. Swartwelder, a surgeon, gave a brief treatise on Union Yuban in which he stated that green beans were toasted in camp kettles for 15 minutes or more, and the results (which would sometimes very nearly be charcoal) pulverized with rifle butts or flat boulders. Owing to the Southern blockade, Confederate coffee-drinkers generally had to resort to substitutes brewed from peanuts, potatoes, peas, corn, or rye.

The Village Tinsmith's large coffeepot holds 20 eight-ounce cups. It comes with a fully wired spout, rim and handle, the last riveted with lead-free solder.

Price: $45.

Instant Coffee

Mayonnaise, which is named for Napoleon's army cook, is said to have been whipped up during the emperor's Russian campaign out of the ration of eggs and vinegar left in his larder. Although it was developed in an effort to make soldiers' rations less bulky, according to one account, what Napoleon was to mayonnaise, U.S. Grant was to instant coffee. Documents in the National Archives reveal that the beverage was prepared as a paste that, already containing sugar and milk, required only hot water from the soldier making it.

Mucket

Each of us had a small, tin kettle holding three pints or so, fitted with a tight cover. We called them muckets for want of a better name ... I believe almost any of us would throw away a blanket before he would his mucket.

— Oliver W. Norton, Army letters, 1861-1865.

This combination mug and pot measures 5 inches high by 4 inches in diameter. Its hinged lid is riveted with lead-free solder.

Price: $26.

Peach Can Boiler

A replica of a camp improvisation measuring 5 inches high by 4 inches in diameter.

Price: $12.

Other mess tinware replicated by the Village Tinsmith includes a teapot, an officer's cup, a "Berdan Sharpshooter's Mess Tin," and much more.

English Mess Tin

A mess tin, a copy of a museum artifact, replicates an English mess tin purchased by the Confederate government. Also manufactured in the U.S., these mess tins were used by the 6th, 7th and 9th New York Volunteers.

Price: $95.

Catalog specializing in period tinware available.

The Village Tinsmithing Works
P.O. Box 189
Randolph, OH 44265
Phone: 330-325-9101

Utensils

A leading Civil War sutler offers several varieties of period flatware, including bone and wooden handled knives and forks (the latter available with either three or four tines); and fiddle-back patterned tea and tablespoons that have been silver-plated.

Catalog of "Civil War Military Goods" available.

John A. Zaharias, Sutler
P.O. Box 31152
St. Louis, MO 63131
Phone: 314-966-2829
Order Line: 800-966-2829

Patent Camp Stove

A camp stove patented in 1864 is being faithfully replicated by Patrick M. Cunningham of Madison, Indiana. Mr. Cunningham, who has been practicing his craft since the mid-1980s, is a dedicated artisan professionally concerned with the ethics of accurately replicating historical artifacts.

Cunningham's stove is a remarkable example in a small but growing inventory of Civil War replicas. Its prototype, depicted, was produced from the U.S. Patent Office application submitted by George A. Higgins of New York in 1861 and which reads in part:

The object of this invention is to obtain a stove of the simplest construction, which, with its necessary fixtures ... may, when not required for use, be packed within a small compass, and the several parts when in use be capable of being so arranged that a large amount of cooking may be done.

According to *The Watchdog*, a quarterly devoted to furthering the authenticity of Civil War replicas, the Patent Camp Stove consists of a "sturdy double boiler mounted atop a small firebox. Affixed to that are a bake oven, a broiler, and a flat surfaced flue atop which coffee pots and other cooking vessels can be made to boil merrily."

Price: $600.

Literature and price list available.

P. M. Cunningham, Tinner
402 East Main Street
Madison, IN 47250
Phone: 812-273-4193

Regulation Field Medical Case

(Pat. January, 1862)

As shown in Lord's *Encyclopedia*, this black medical case is fully lined in red felt and constructed over a lightweight wooden frame. It contains pockets with a leather closure on each to contain small items. A long, removable shoulder strap has buckle adjustment and a shoulder pad. Inside the large leather flap, a label indicates the case's patent date and lists its original contents, including adhesive plaster, digitalis, and opium.

Dimensions: 6½ inches high by 12½ inches wide by 7½ inches deep.

Price: $189.

Ho! ho! old saw bones, here you come, Yes, when the rebels whack us. You are always ready with your traps, To mangle, saw, and hack us.

Dixie Leather Works
306 N. 7th Street
Paducah, KY 42001
Phone: 502-442-1058
Fax: 502-442-1049
Order Line: 800-888-5183

Medical Instrument Roll-Up Kit

Civil War surgeons' field cases were produced by the Geo. Tiemann Co. of 63 Chatham Street in New York. Bearing this company's name in gold leaf, Dixie Leather Works' medical roll-up kits have different-sized loops to hold such period medical instruments as tenaculums, bistouries, and trocars against a red suede lining.

Prices: $38 for a kit measuring 4 by 7 inches, $46 for one measuring 6 by 9 inches.

The Hospital Steward John McEvoy's Knapsack

(Pat. January, 1862)

A replica of the medical steward's field knapsack depicted in Dr. Gordon Damann's *Medical Instruments and Equipment, Vol. II.* The knapsack consists of a lightweight wooden frame covered in black, weatherproof canvas. Consistent with the original, the unit's top opens to an array of slotted compartments for the storage of medical bandages and bottles. A side door opens to reveal two sliding drawers. All straps are made of top-grain cowhide.

Dimensions: 15 inches high by 13 inches wide by 6¼ inches deep.

Price: $291.50.

Medical Corps saddlebag and surgeon's valise also available.

Catalog of "'Hard-To-Find' 19th Century Military Goods & Reproduction Living History Accessories," $6 U.S., $10 abroad.

Dixie Leather Works
306 N. 7th Street
Paducah, KY 42001
Phone: 502-442-1058
Fax: 502-442-1049
Order Line: 800-888-5183

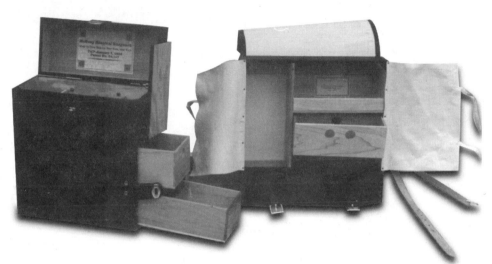

Small Medicine Tin Labels

Pre-Civil War medical treatments focused on the regulation of the body's vast Mississippi Missouri of fluid as it coursed through veins, bowels, and kidneys. Chief among the engineers enlisted in the cause of proper fluid dynamics was calomel, a mercury-based cathartic responsible for much poisoning among those it helped purge. Opiates were administered promiscuously in the cause of painkilling, with laudanum and morphine achieving effective results. Many such drugs were available as patent medicines, to which the eminent Dr. Oliver Wendell Holmes, Sr. referred when he chastised the public for insisting "on being poisoned" by them. Nor were the doctors who prescribed powerful medicines exempt from his scorn: "If the whole *materia medica*, as now used, would sink to the bottom of the sea," he advised them, "it would be all the better for mankind, and all the worse for the fishes"

Little more than a treatment for naked Civil War medicine tins, reproduced labels for "Cephalic Pills," (an apparently broad-spectrum headache remedy that will "Cure Sick Headache, Cure Nervous Headache, Cure All Kinds of Headache") and "Turner's Tic Douloureux, or Universal Neuralgia Pill," are available.

Price: Five for $1

Free price list of cartridges, ammunition boxes, labels and souvenirs available.

Cartridges Unlimited
4320-A Hartford St.
St. Louis, MO 63116
Phone: 314-664-4332

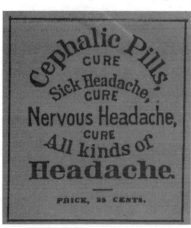

Medical Tin

A black painted medical can closely resembling that made by the Village Tinsmith appears in Lord's *Encyclopedia* marked "Pilulae Quinae Surphatis."

Prices: Small medical tin, 8.5 centimeters by 3.5 centimeters by 3.5 centimeters, $8; medium medical tin, 9 centimeters by 5 centimeters by 5 centimeters, $10; large medical tin 10.5 centimeters by 5 centimeters by 5 centimeters, $13.

A round chloroform and a rectangular "spirits fermenti" tin are also available.

Wooden Stethoscope

Induction examinations given during the Civil War were cursory affairs that sometimes involved no doctors at all. If a man worked for a living, had all his visible organs and appendages and wasn't apparently sick he was ready for duty. "If we were not floored nor showed any other signs of inconvenience," wrote a New Jersey recruit, "we were pronounced in good condition and ordered to fall in on the other side of the room where…we amused ourselves by grinning at each other."

Price: $30.

Leech Box

Hirudo Medicinalis, the type of leech used to bleed sick soldiers, were quartered in sliding, punctured tins.

Dimensions: 4 inches long by 2¼ inches wide by 1 inch deep.

Price: $15.

"Kidney bean" canteen, invalid feeding cup, and bleeding bowl also obtainable.

Catalog specializing in period tinware available.

The Village Tinsmithing Works
P.O. Box 189
Randolph, OH 44265
Phone: 330-325-9101

PATENT MEDICINES

Wakefield's Blackberry Balsam

The bowels are of more consequence than the brains.

—A wartime axiom.

The most frequently encountered of all Civil War maladies, chronic diarrhea was responsible for more deaths than was combat. At a loss for ways to treat the condition, doctors resorted to everything from overdoses of drugs to "rectal cauterization." Perhaps overlooked was the fact that since 1848, the Wakefield company had been offering a treatment certain to be more pleasant than any of these.

Price: $10.60 for 6 fluid ounces.

Father John's Throat Medicine

Exposure to the elements brought on by insufficient or worn clothing, tents, and blankets brought colds, bronchitis, and pneumonia to Confederate soldiers especially. Dr. John's had been around for seven years when, in 1862, an Iowan would confide to his diary that: "Uniforms in [were in a] bad light—feet wet and cold and patriotism down to zero."

Contains no alcohol or habit-forming drugs.

Price: $9.40

Catalog available, $4

Cumberland General Store
#1 Highway 68
Crossville, TN 38555
Fax: 615-456-1211
Order Line: 800-334-4640

Dunbar's Bitters and Patent Medicine Flyer

Complete with glowing testimonials.

"General Catalog" available," $2.

Amazon Drygoods
2218 E. 11th Street
Davenport, IA 52803-3760
Phone: 319-322-6800
Fax: 319-322-4003
Order Line: 800-798-7979

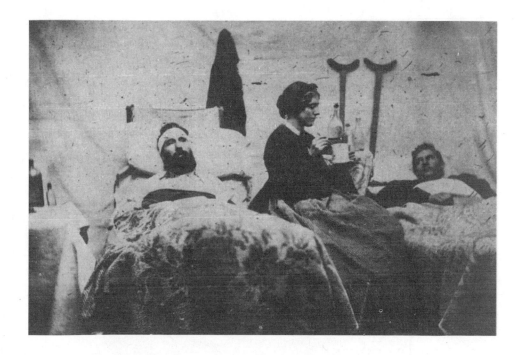

MEDICAL & SURGICAL BOOKS

Of the approximately half-million men killed during the Civil War, only about a third were felled by direct enemy action. Disease was the biggest killer. Among Union forces there were some 400,000 cases of injuries and wounds and nearly 600,000 cases of sickness. Worse than that, it has been estimated that each of the 600,000 fighting men mobilized by the Confederate States fell victim to injury and disease approximately six times during the war, producing a total patient count of more than 3,600,000.

The demands were of a magnitude never before experienced. To help meet this crisis—as well as to reflect all that was being learned from it—a library of medical and surgical books was published during the course of the war. Grouped into "The American Civil War Medical Series" and "The American Civil War Surgery Series," a limited-printing of facsimiles of these works are available from Norman Publishing of San Francisco.

The American Civil War Medical Series is comprised of thirteen works set into twelve volumes. It constitutes a reprinting of the rare original editions page for page, in their original size and on acid-free paper. Moreover, the volumes of The American Civil War Medical Series are bound in colored cloth bindings similar to those of the Civil War era. Included are:

Hints on the Preservation of Health in Armies

by John Ordronaux, New York, 1861. 142 pages.

The first American book on military hygiene, this edition is bound with the *Manual of Instructions for Military Surgeons*, an 1863 volume by the same author and publisher.

Price: $45.

Resources of Southern Fields and Forests: Medical, Economical & Agricultural

by Francis P. Porcher, Richmond, 1863.

Reminiscent of a survival manual, *Resources* has been credited with maintaining the Southern war effort for many months beyond what would have been possible had it not been written. Using this 601-page reference, Confederate medical officers were able to defy the blockade of their ports by supplying their medicinal needs through the preparation of drugs from plants native to the South.

Price: $75.

Confederate States Medical & Surgical Journal

Richmond: January 1864 - February 1865.

This, the only medical journal published by the Confederacy, is considered by Norman Publishing to be "virtually impossible to find complete in its original printing." The January and February numbers were the only ones issued. Although printed and ready for distribution, the March number was destroyed during the burning of Richmond on April 2 in 1865.

Price: $95.

Illustrated Manual of Operative Surgery & Surgical Anatomy

by Claude Bernard and Charles Huette. Edited, with notes and additions by William H. Van Buren and Charles E. Isaacs.

First published in New York in 1861. This book is described by Norman Publishing as "the most elaborately illustrated of surgical manuals published during the Civil War, with 88 plates depicting operations and surgical instruments. This American edition for Civil War surgeons was the best version ever published of these widely translated manuals."

Price: $125.

A Treatise on Hygiene

by William A. Hammond, Philadelphia, 1863.

Organized into three sections, "On the Examination of Recruits," "Of the Agents Inherent in the Organism Which Affect the Hygienic Condition of Man," and "Of Agents External to the Organism Which Act Upon the Health of Man," Hammond's 74-page *Treatise* rigorously promotes strict hygienic practices.

Price: $60.

The American Civil War Surgery Series

The second series, on American Civil War surgery, reprints the first editions of the six manuals written by Union surgeons and issued during the war, together with six wartime manuals written by Confederate surgeons. Not bound as authentically as volumes in the medical series, the surgical series' books are printed on acid-free paper and smyth sewn. The Union manuals are bound in high-quality blue cloth with black spine labels, and like many of the original editions issued for Union surgeons, are stamped with "U.S. Army Medical Department" on the upper corner. Confederate Manuals are plainly bound to match original editions. The series includes *A Manual for Military Surgery, Prepared for Use of the Confederate States Army*, the only Confederate surgical manual that is extensively illustrated.

Prices: The entire set of the American Civil War Surgery Series is available for $495 postpaid in the continental United States. (Outside the continental U.S. there is an additional cost for shipping and handling.) ISBN 0-930405-46-3. Prices for individual volumes are obtainable from the publisher.

The entire set of The American Civil War Medical Series can be purchased for $595 postpaid in the continental United States. ISBN 0-930405-45-5.

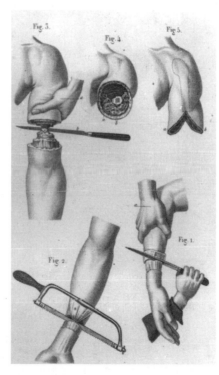

Both sets may be purchased for the advance payment of $995 postpaid in the continental United States.

Norman Publishing has also made available on a limited basis facsimile editions of Civil War surgical instrument catalogs. These are comprised of Snowden and Brother's *Illustrated Wholesale Catalogue of Surgical and Dental Instruments, Elastic Trusses and Medical Saddle Bags* [etc.] (Philadelphia, 1860), which is bound with John Weiss and Sons' *Catalogue of Surgical Instruments, Apparatus, Appliances*, etc. (London, 1863). The latter has been included because many mid-nineteenth-century surgeons and hospitals ordered their equipment from English suppliers.

Price: The surgical instrument catalogs are obtainable for $150 a pair.

Printings of all editions have been limited to 750 copies each.

Brochure available.

Norman Publishing
Third Floor, 720 Market Street
San Francisco, CA 94102-2502
Phone: 415-781-6402
E-mail: orders@jnorman.com
Order line: 800-544-9359

COMFORTS, CONSOLATIONS & AMUSEMENTS

MUSIC

I don't think we can have an army without music.

—Robert E. Lee

Bugle

Campaigning on the Virginia Peninsula early in the war, U.S. Gen. Daniel Butterfield whistled a tune he couldn't get out of his mind. He repeated it for his bugler, who, after they revised it somewhat, wrote the melody down on the back of an envelope. Following Gen. Butterfield's instruction, the bugler played the new song at day's end, as did those in other regiments who heard it. After going west with the army, "Taps" soon became regulation.

Legendary Arms' Civil War bugle is a solid brass replica.

Catalog available.

Legendary Arms, Inc.
P.O. Box 29
Dunellen, NJ 08812-0299
Phone: 908-424-8636
Fax: 908-424-2303
Order Line: 800-528-2767

Maple Fife

While the numbers of regimental bands were greatly reduced after 1862, fife and drum corps generally remained throughout the war. These outfits were capable of great inspiration according to Francis A. Lord, particularly when "in a great army stretching out for miles, a single bugle-note gave the signal, and then, as by magic, from every direction broke out the accelerating roll of drums, the screech of fifes, the blare of bugles."

Dixie Leather Works' maple fife sports the same tapered shape as that shown in Lord's *Encyclopedia*. Moreover, its long brass end ferrules are claimed by the company catalog to be "appropriate for both the eighteenth and nineteenth centuries."

Price: $14.50

Catalog of "Hard-To-Find' 19th Century Military Goods & Reproduction Living History Accessories," $6 within the U.S., $10 abroad.

Dixie Leather Works
306 N. 7th Street
Paducah, KY 42001
Phone: 502-442-1058
Fax: 502-442-1049
Order Line: 800-888-5183

Regimental Brass Band

The drums are loudly beating
and the pipes do sweetly play.
If it weren't for that, Polly my dear
With you I'd gladly stay.

—The Pogues, "Gentleman Soldier," Rum, Sodomy and
the Lash, 1985.

These were the very reasons given by one U.H. Farr as he recalled why he "stepped into the ranks with the others" to join the 17th Indiana Regiment in 1862. Despite the liveliness of its airs, the military band plays a solemn mass to the love of danger and comradeship within young men's souls.

But the brass band's quick-stepping siren songs were not limited to enlistment rallies. In May of 1861 the U.S. War Department decreed that each infantry or artillery regiment could form a twenty-four-man band, an offer that nearly three-quarters of all regiments had complied with by that winter. In addition to sundown serenades, the bands played while on the march, during dress parades, and at formal reviews and funerals. Citing a need for economy, the U.S. Adjutant General required that all volunteer regimental brass ensembles be disbanded in July of '62. But the order doing so provided for brigade-level replacements, and so the marches, operas, and parade of such popular favorites as "Hard Crackers, Come

Again No More," and "Yankee Doodle Dandy" continued. It was not uncommon for the ensembles to be booked to play the front lines, as they did at the March 31, 1865 Battle of Five Forks. In the midst of the fray, they were observed there by Gen. Horace Porter "playing 'Nellie Bly' as cheerily as if furnishing music for a picnic."

The Saxton's Coronet Band's recreation of a Civil War brass ensemble is the product of ten years' research. According to their literature, this commitment extends to the band's strict use of American-made instruments from the 1850s and early 1860s to perform music that has been "meticulously hand copied note for note from band books used … in the mid-nineteenth century." The authentically garbed ensemble can be hired to play the music appropriate for Union or Confederate balls, stage shows, reenactments, civic ceremonies, concerts, and parades. In addition, two cassette tapes, "Saxton's Regimental Band Presents the 4th Kentucky Regimental Band" and "Saxton's Coronet Band Presents a Grand Military Ball," are available for $10 each.

For information regarding bookings and tapes, contact:

Saxton's Coronet Band
341 Mooreland Avenue
Harrodsburg, KY 40330
Phone: 606-734-0028

Johnny Shiloh
Was a Drummer

Near the start of World War I, a brigadier general retired who had long since been a legend of the Civil War.

In the spring of 1861, nine-year-old John Joseph Clem chased after regiments passing through his Newark, Ohio, hometown until he could convince the 22nd Massachusetts to take him on as a drummer boy. At first, a hat had to be passed among the unit's officers to supply the lad with his monthly pay of $13 while comrades-in-arms provided a sawed-down rifle and a "Just-Like-Dad's" suit of army blue. But these brotherly indulgences would be forever altered by the 1862 Battle of Shiloh, for it was there that Clem's reputation was made the moment his drum played its own one-note dirge when smashed by a round of enemy artillery. As a result, the brave "Johnny Shiloh" was officially enrolled in the 22nd, and received his pay directly from the government.

Notable as were the events of Shiloh, neither did Clem's derring-do nor his nicknames end with them. In September '63, the boy avoided the capture that befell many of his fellow soldiers at Chickamauga by shooting the sesech officer into whose grasp he was about to fall. This act won him two citations: the first a promotion to lance corporal; and the second an elevation to fame as "the Drummer Boy of Chickamauga" as proclaimed by newspapers throughout the North. It might also be said that around this time Clem gave himself a promotion when he changed his name from John Joseph to John Lincoln.

The month following Chickamauga, Clem's rate of ascent stalled somewhat when he was taken prisoner by Confederate cavalry. Still

continued on page 97...

Drums

Beat, beat! drums!

—Walt Whitman, in a Union recruiting poem first published September 28, 1861.

After recruitment, regimental "calls" were an important and continuous fact of army life in both camp and field. As unwelcome as was the sound of a drum call for yet another detail to form in front of the adjutant's tent, as Francis A. Lord states in his book *They Fought for the Union*, such calls were associated with "much of the genuine romance of camp life."

For troops on the march, the bass drum generally brought up the rear. As it was both heavy and unwieldy, the drummer was likely to be more footsore than those soldiers for whom he beat time.

Regulations ordained that U.S. Army bass and snare drums be painted with the national coat of arms. However, museum and personal collections reveal that nearly all such drums were devoid of decoration

Johnny Shiloh, continued

only twelve, Clem was released in a prisoner exchange, but not until after the southerners advertised him as an example of "what sore straits the Yankees are driven, when they have to send their babies to fight us." That January, Gen. George Thomas attached Johnny to his own staff as a mounted orderly. He served in this position until September 19, 1864, when he was discharged from the army.

President Grant was naturally well aware of Chickamauga's famous drummer and appointed the young man to West Point. But, poorly-educated as Clem was, he repeatedly failed to pass the entrance examination—a situation that Grant remedied by simply making him a 2nd lieutenant. This second military career didn't end until Clem's retirement in 1915, when he was the last Civil War veteran on army rolls. The legendary John Joseph Shiloh Lincoln Clem, Drummer Boy of Chickamauga, died in San Antonio, Texas, in 1936, and was buried in Arlington National Cemetery.

other than for the five-pointed stars sometimes tacked or nailed into their shells. Occasionally, military drums carried by state units would bear the state's coat of arms.

Handmade reproductions of such Civil War drums are available from the Eames Drum Company of Saugus, Massachusetts. They are suitably plain, with maple-stained shells and red hoops surrounding weatherproof heads. Drum cords, slings, sticks, and tension tugs are also obtainable, as are calfskin heads and bass drum beaters.

Bass drums are available 16 inches high by 20 inches in diameter and 18 inches high by 22 inches in diameter. Snare drums can be had in four sizes ranging from 10 inches high to 14 inches in diameter to 16 inches high by 16 inches in diameter.

Brochure obtainable.

Eames Drum Company
229 Hamilton Street
Saugus, Mass. 01906
Phone: 617-233-1404

CAMP INSTRUMENTS

While both regimental and brigade bands were welcomed by troops starved for outside entertainment, camp music was usually the province of individual soldiers. As most units on either side included a talented fiddler or two, such melodies as "The Arkansas Traveler" and "Billy in the Low Grounds" were well underway before the request for them was completed. Fiddlers drew ready accompaniment by banjo players, and the jew's harp players who were around in even greater numbers.

Jew's Harp

A popular folk instrument at the time of the Civil War, the Jew's harp's accessibility and size made its use by soldiers inevitable. Now more accurately termed the jaw or mouth harp, its players twanged its spring in time to such songs as "Johnny Fill Up the Bowl" just like Billy-be-damned.

Price: $2.75.

Catalog of Early American frontier items, $2.

Panther Primitives
P.O. Box 32
Normantown, WV 25267
Phone: 304-462-7718
Order Line: 800-467-2684

Violins

Violins underwent an important change during the period extending from 1820 to 1840. By the time that violinist Ole Bull enchanted the audience that heard the Fifth Symphony at the New York Philharmonic's premier performance on December 7, 1842, the necks of newly made violins had lengthened, growing from 12¼ inches to 13 inches in length. This alteration inspired some makers to commit the fraud of scribing a line in the necks of their new, 13-inch violins to convey the impression that they were older (and more valuable) instruments that had undergone modernization. Most violins available during the Civil War were themselves copies of older Stainers and Stradivariuses, with many incorporating the falsely scribed 13-inch necks. The Wunder Banjo Company will make such violins by hand and reconfigure older models to replicate typical Civil War varieties. To accomplish the same end with modern violins, the Maryland firm begins by first stripping these of their plastic parts and high-gloss lacquer finishes.

Prices: Handmade replica Civil War violins begin at $700. Old violins correctly set up start at $350. Prices for modifying your violin will be quoted on an individual basis.

Free catalog available.

Wunder Banjo Company
Phone: 800-891-6541

Banjos

In those dim, Georgia-Pacific-paneled halls of the American memory, banjo music is thought to be about as Appalachian as musket fire. The fact is that prior to the Civil War, the instrument was more likely to be played in Brooklyn than on the Blue Ridge. The banjo has an African—and therefore a plantation slave—genesis; but even before the Revolution, white actors with burnt-cork on their faces were performing with banjos in travelling circus acts and as a part of the "Ethiopian Delineator's" bag of tricks. By 1843, the "Virginia Minstrels," the first full-length blackface show was playing large cities throughout the U.S. and Europe; and in 1857, 3,000 New Yorkers crowded into the Old Chinese Assembly Room on Broadway to hear a battle-of-the-banjos between representatives of different city neighborhoods. By this time the banjo was well established in Anglo-American culture as a popular instrument. It was readily carried to the Great American War, as scores of camp photographs attest.

The Wunder Banjo Company was born of George Wunderlich's frustra-tion in trying to achieve the correct Civil War-era sound on modern banjos. This led him to conduct research on period instruments at the Smithsonian Institution, the Metropolitan Museum of Art, the Missouri Historical Society, and elsewhere to ascertain the original material and techniques used to produce nineteenth-century banjos. These are now faithfully employed to make his replicas, which are tested against originals to ensure the correct period tone, character, and volume of music.

Prices: "William Boucher 1846 Banjo," "William Boucher 1846 Plain-Style," "Early Home-Made," "Sweeney-Style Tackhead," and "1850s Concert" banjos are available for $505, $495, $405, $435, and $560 respectively. The Wunder company is also a source for two reprinted banjo instruction books, the *Briggs Banjo Instructor of 1855,* and the *Converse Method for the Banjo of 1865,* for $16 and $18 respectively.

Free catalog available.

Wunder Banjo Co.
Phone: 800-891-6541

This 1860s concert banjo is a copy of one by an unknown maker dated 1864.

Wunder Banjo's 1846 Boucher style banjo has the inlaid fingerboard typical of the 1850s and '60s.

GAMES

Playing Cards

Bristol threw down a flyspecked ten,
"Theah," he said in the soft, sweet drawl
That could turn as hard as a Minie-ball,
"This heah day is my lucky day,
And Shepley nevah could play piquet,"
He stretched his arms in a giant yawn.
"Gentlemen, when are we movin' on?
I have no desire for a soldier's end,
While I still have winnin's that I can spend,
And they's certain appointments with certain ladies
Which I'd miss right smart if I went to Hades,
Especially one little black-eyed charmer
Whose virtue, one hopes, is her only armor,
So if Sergeant Wingate's mended his saddle
I suggest that we all of us now skedaddle
To employ a term that the Yankees favor —"

— Stephen Vincent Benét, *John Brown's Body*, 1927

Poker was the game in most regiments, but twenty-one, faro, cribbage, euchre, keno, and "chuck-a-luck" were also played, seemingly, whenever two or more soldiers could produce a deck. *The Civil War Collector's Encyclopedia* notes that in the 150th Pennsylvania, "throwing the papers" was the "absorbing occupation" of soldiers and officers alike—" the former risking his scanty allowance as the latter their liberal stipend."

The replacement of traditional playing-card iconography with military and patriotic figures was fashionable. "Union Playing Cards," a deck sold by The American Card Company, substituted eagles, shields, stars, and flags for conventional suits and curiously mated "a colonel" with "The Goddess of Liberty" to serve as kings and queens. An example of Confederate playing cards illustrated in Lord's *Encyclopedia* shows them to have "a stand-of-arms design, while the cards themselves each bear a portrait of a different Confederate general or cabinet member."

Similarly, U.S. Games Systems' "Union and Confederate Military Leaders Playing Cards Decks" each bear the engravings of fifty-two principals of the contending sides. According to their current publisher, the decks are facsimiles of a pair published in 1863 by a New York house named M. Nelson. In the absence of any southern playing card manufacturers, the Yankee publisher was unconcerned about memorializing the enemy's leaders on his pasteboards.

Price: $12, the set.

Free catalog of playing cards and games available.

U.S. Games Systems
179 Ludlow Street
Stamford, CT 06902
Phone: 203-353-8400
Fax: 203-353-8431
Order Line: 800-544-2637

Checkerboard

While chess was rarely played, checkers was a popular game among soldiers and sailors. Checkerboards typical of those used during the mid-nineteenth century are available from Indiana cabinetmaker, Michael L. Lester. Hand-planed and painted with one of two combinations of traditional color schemes, the poplar boards are available in red oxide on dark green, or yellow ochre on red oxide. Spoke-shave moldings are applied with cut nails.

Prices: 12-inch square, $48; 12 inches by 20 inches, $58; plus $6 each for shipping.

Folk Art Studios
611 West 12th Street
Bloomington, IN 47404
Phone: 812-336-5575

Wooden Dice

While the most popular game of dice in camp was craps, a close second was "sweet cloth" (or "bird cage"), in which players bet on the number to be rolled from a cup. Lord's *Encyclopedia* notes that Civil War dice were "crude and of much smaller size than in common use today."

Catalog of "Civil War Era Items," 75¢.

Kentwood Sutlery and Manufacturing
P.O. Box 88201
Kentwood, MI 49518
Phone: 616-531-7645

TOBACCO ITEMS

Tobacco Road: "Stogies" took their name from the men who preferred to smoke them—the Conestoga wagon drivers who plied the National Road between Baltimore, Maryland, and Columbus, Ohio, early in the nineteenth century.

Stogie Cigars

Never did Raleighs contain a coupon so valuable as Special Order No. 191. Issued on September 9, 1862 during Lee's first invasion of the Union, the order clearly described the Army of Northern Virginia's whereabouts in regard to Lee's plan to divide his forces between Maryland and Virginia. As the maneuvers detailed in 191 were to begin on the 10th, the order was immediately dispatched to those commanders directly involved. Major Gen. Daniel Harvey (D.H.) Hill, who was to act as Longstreet's rear guard, somehow received two copies—one through his corps commander Stonewall Jackson, and another direct. Hill held on to Jackson's copy, but in the confusion before departure, the other found its way into service as some officer's cigar wrapper.

Then, whoever enlisted Special Order No. 191 in the cause of pure smoking satisfaction dropped the cigars.

On the night of the 12th, two soldiers from the 27th Indiana Regiment, which had quickly come up behind Lee, were in their Maryland bivouac. In camp, they spied the weather-stained bundle of cigars as it lay on the ground somewhere outside Frederick. Reading the wrapper on their remarkable find, the soldiers soon became aware of its prizewinning potential.

The next morning, McClellan was aware of it as well: "My general idea is to cut the enemy in two and beat him in detail," he said, seemingly claiming Lee's tactical risk as a personal credit. However, Lee's daring was met by McClellan's usual caution, and despite the advantage the orders provided, the latter advanced slowly, suspicious that they were part of an elaborate trap. At the battle of South Mountain on the 14th, McClellan's army forced Lee's withdrawal. On the following day however, troops under Confederate Gen. Lafayette McLaws obtained the unconditional surrender of the Federal garrison at Harper's Ferry.

While the stage was thus being set for the Battle of Antietam,

M. Marsh & Sons Factory, 1856. Mifflin Marsh stands in the doorway.

Mifflin Marsh was rolling his cigars in Wheeling, West Virginia some 200 miles away. Mr. Marsh's stogies were the relatively long and thin cigars favored by the conestoga wagon drivers who plied the National Road during the mid-1800s. Although today's milder Marsh-Wheelings greatly differ from the rough, hand-rolled cigars of that time, the company's "Olde Style" stogies are rounded, per their 1840s forebears.

Order form available.

M. Marsh & Son
915 Market Street
P.O. Box 6604
Wheeling, WV 26003
Phone: 800-624-5495
Fax: 304-232-4472

Kinnikinnick

In its various forms, the word "kinnikinnick" comes from the Cree dialect of the Algonquin language and means "what is mixed." What was mixed by the Indians was originally dried sumac leaves together with other ingredients. As a name for smoking mixtures used by both red men and white, kinnikinnick was widely employed throughout the nineteenth century, and sutlers (the traveling merchants who followed and helped supply both armies) sold Kinnikinnick-brand tobacco to Civil War troops for a dollar a pound.

The Crazy Crow Trading Post offers several blends of Indian kinnikinnick, loosely replicating what might have been smoked early in the nineteenth century: Northern Plains, "a mild blend of … tobacco leaves, and herbs common to the Indians of the upper Missouri River country": Eastern Woodlands, "a … blend of tobacco, roots, and bark preferred by the Indian forest dwellers of the Eastern United States"; Comanche Straight, "a non-tobacco blend of herbs, bark, and leaves from the Southern Plains"; and Great Lakes Straight, "an all-herbal blend based upon an old 'good medicine' recipe. The herbs that are used were common to the Indian people of the midwestern woodlands, the Appalachians, and the Ozarks."

Catalog, $3.

Crazy Crow Trading Post
P.O. Box 314-AMS
Denison, TX 75020
Phone: 903-786-2287

PIPES

Who can find words to tell the story of the soldier's affection for his faithful briar-root pipe! As the cloudy incense of the weed rises in circling wreaths about his head, as he hears the murmuring of the fire and watches the glowing and fading of the embers, and feels the comfort of the hour pervading his mortal frame, what bliss!

—Carlton McCarthy, Pvt., 2nd Company Richmond Howitzers, in his book, *Detailed Minutiae of Soldier Life in the Army of Northern Virginia, 1861-1865*, 1882.

The American philosopher George Santayana said that those who cannot remember the past are condemned to repeat it. Conversely, those who cannot forget the past are often condemned to reenact it.

Civil War soldiers relished their pipes. They often bought pipes of clay or briar from sutlers or—while on the march—fashioned a smoke out of a corncob or cherry branch. So while it befits a Civil War reenactor to smoke a pipe, there's something about the fire of their miniature furnaces—or the sense of wholeness that returns in the wake of their curling smoke—that recommends the pipe as an icon for the war itself.

Pipe carver Peter Evans is insightful in the manner of pipe smokers. He notes how reenactors have taken to reversing their kepis in battle—an affectation more likely to be found among inner-city homeboys

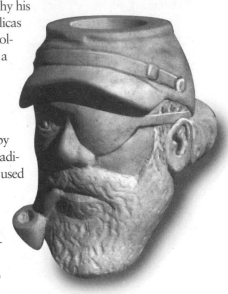

than Winslow Homer subjects. Saying "Many beautiful pipes came out of that tragic war," Mr. Evans also has a keen awareness of the inventive designs that war-wrought pipes display. That is why his one-of-a-kind replicas can resemble "a soldier's weary face, a wind-riffled flag, an authentic gun mechanism, [or] creases in a uniform." Made as by soldiers— with traditional hand tools used over the course of days—these pipes are considered to be of heirloom quality by their maker, who signs each one.

For their Civil War pipes, Mr. Evans' customers can choose from a variety of materials, stems, and shapes. Moreover, their styles can either draw upon a suggested list of carved images (flags, eagles, shields, etc.), or be sculpted into the shape of "anything you imagine." A review of Mr. Evans' brochure shows his pipes tending in the direction of carved briars and meerschaums (sometimes bearing the likenesses of historic Civil War figures); of replicas of the pipes smoked by those figures; or more conventional Civil-War briars. Here is an example of each.

Carved Briar

This pipe is a standard briar with a bent stem bearing three images (the seal of the Commonwealth of Virginia is visible), with scrollwork overall on its bowl and inscriptions on the rear of the bowl and right stem side. Reflecting the importance soldiers placed on individualizing their pipes, it is the replica of an actual Civil War pipe made in Maryland.

Chindangler

A curved pipe that is characterized as the "soldier's standard briar."

Carved Meerschaum

The bowl of a standard meerschaum with a single carved image and straight stem.

Buford's Pipe

When Union General John Buford encountered the enemy advancing on Gettysburg from the northwest, he immediately dismounted his cavalry unit to hold McPherson Ridge until reinforcing infantry could arrive. Buford's immediate grasp of the importance of the junction where he made his stand is another of those actions without which the Federal victory at Gettysburg might not have occurred.

Peter Evans' Buford pipe replicates the one smoked by the character portraying the general in the film "Gettysburg." It too is individually handcarved out of a solid block of aged briar. The pipe has a traditional hard-rubber stem and bears the owner's initials, hand engraved in an ornamental, period script. It is, according to one customer, "truly a work of art ... regardless of the fact that a Yankee general smoked it." This Tennessean may have been more comfortable with Evans' lion-headed pipe, the same leonine meerschaum smoked by Gen. Longstreet in "Gettysburg."

Prices vary according to the complexity of the pipe ordered, and include $5.99 for a plain clay pipe and $324.95 for a bowl bearing three carved images. The Buford and Longstreet pipes each cost $99—the former including initials, the latter a fitted case.

Brochure and price list available.

Peter Evans Pipes
285 West Mashta Drive
Department W
Key Biscayne, FL 33149
Phone: 305-361-5589

LETTERS HOME

1860s Writing Box

Here is paper, ink, pen and pencil. What shall be done with this pile of treasure?

—Carlton McCarthy, Pvt., 2nd Company Richmond Howitzers, *Detailed Minutiae of Soldier Life in the Army of Northern Virginia, 1861-1865, 1882.*

For stationery, soldiers sometimes procured anything handy—the backs of military forms, used brown paper, and the reversed leaves of letters from home. However, this shouldn't be taken to mean that real letter-paper wasn't obtainable, for many types were marketed during the war years. Such stationery was often distinguished by its use of patriotic emblems—flags, swords, eagles, cannon, and sentries clad in blue or gray.

Letters home were one of the primary comforts of camp life. As they required soldiers to have writing implements, stamps, and a sturdy, flat surface in addition to stationery, officers in particular made use of a writing box. Replicated from an officer's original, the House of Kirk's example is available in cherry or walnut. It contains an accurate assembly of fittings, including a blown-glass ink bottle, a candle and candle holder, a hand-turned pen, and reproduction stamps, stationery, envelopes, and military papers. Each box is numbered and signed by its maker, and may be engraved with its owner's name.

Price: $200.

Price sheet for Civil War replica writing box, stamps, stationery, and ammunition boxes available.

House of Kirk
9380 Collins Parkway
P.O. Box 808
New Market, VA 22844
Phone: 540-740-8296
Fax: 540-740-4459

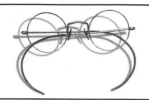
Vulcanite Pocket Combs

Civil War military issue did not include combs, and most of those that survive are of the small, folding variety. Francis A. Lord claims this is so because the folding combs were likely to be preserved, while their rigid counterparts — which he believes to have been in greater use — were carried into postwar life. There, this theory presumably runs, the combs became toothless veterans and were discarded.

The Ace pocket combs depicted here are included as the result of an artifact hunter's divulgence, that (in a

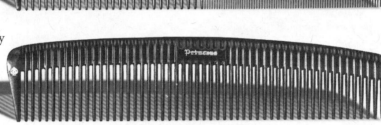

remarkable, movie-title-like dovetailing of the past, the present, the singular, and the banal) this brand of hard-rubber pocket comb was found in the pockets of Civil War dead. Hard rubber was also called vulcanite and ebonite then, and was used in the manufacture of such items as buttons, flasks, cups, pipes, soap boxes, and syringes in addition to combs.

Available at drug counters in the U.S. and elsewhere.

Toothbrush

In 1863, an engagingly cavalier Englishman, Lt. Col. Arthur Fremantle of Her Majesty's Coldstream Guards, spent his vacation on a tour of Southern home and battle fronts, recording his memorable characterizations of its people, soldiers and commanders. His book, *Three Months in the Southern States*, is therefore rich in detail, as when, whilst he accompanied the Army of Northern Virginia across the Potomac, Fremantle observed that the only uniformity among Southern troops was the toothbrush invariably found stuck into their lapels.

Toothbrushes changed but little from the Civil to the Persian Gulf Wars. Panther Primitives' bone-handled, boar-bristled

example claims to be "exactly as those found among the personal effects of Civil War soldiers."

Price: $5.

Catalog of Early American frontier items, $2.

Panther Primitives
P.O. Box 32
Normantown, WV 25267
Phone: 304-462-7718
Order Line: 800-487-2684

Housewife

Rather than sew anything, most soldiers preferred drawing new clothing or "finding" items momentarily left unguarded by comrades. For those inclined towards mending their clothes —a "housewife," or sewing kit, served their purposes. Typically, Johnny Reb or Billy Yank got their housewives from wives, mothers, sisters, or sweethearts—although soldier's aid societies also made them available. Housewives described in *The Civil War Collector's Encyclopedia* tend to be leather wallets measuring two-to-three-inches square, and containing pockets for the necessary needles, yarn, and thimbles.

Dixie Leather Works' housewife holds buttons, needles and thread. It has three separate outside pockets and measures 5 inches wide by 13 inches long. Specify black or brown leather.

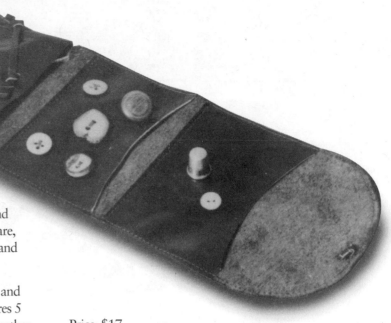

Price: $17.

Bawdy House Tokens

A day's pass of a different kind was the entrée to "Hooker's Headquarters," "Madam Russell's Bake Oven" and other war-zone bordellos for lager beer and a night of what one Massachusetts soldier referred to as "riding a Dutch gal." By 1862, Washington alone had 450 such enterprises, and an estimated 7,500 prostitutes.

Replica whorehouse tokens for Hap's Bath House in New York, and saloons named Swede's, Stella's and Fat Anne's in Chicago, Atlanta and New Orleans respectively, have been cast from original dies.

Price: $3.50 apiece, two for $5.

Wrapper for "Doctor Lynde's French Envelopes (condoms)," also obtainable.

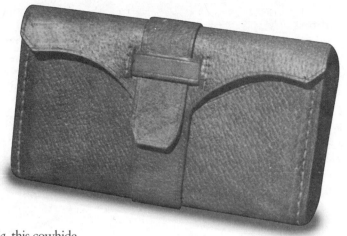

Wallet

Replicating that shown in Lord's *Encyclopedia*, this cowhide wallet measures 6 ¾ by 4 inches.

Price: $20.

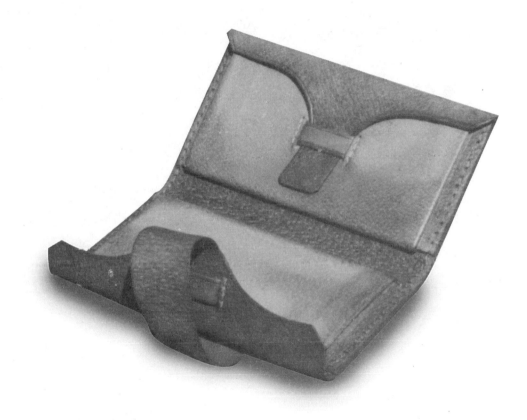

Catalog of "'Hard-To-Find' 19th Century Military Goods & Reproduction Living History Accessories," $6 within the U.S., $10 abroad.

Dixie Leather Works
306 N. 7th Street
Paducah, KY 42001
Phone: 502-442-1058
Fax: 502-442-1049
Order Line: 800-888-5183

Eyeglasses

On the Wilderness battlefield of May 5, 1863, Union Gen. Winfield Scott Hancock's corps was ordered to hold up in the vicinity of Todd's Tavern. But as Hancock and his men had been quick to comply with previous orders, they found themselves miles beyond this point, at a crossroads named Shady Grove Church. So to get into position for what would be a day's fighting against A.P. Hill and another against reinforcements under the command of General James Longstreet, Hancock had to countermarch back to the tavern.

Lee's appearance would soon make this battleground still more torturous and confusing, but at least in those days the *place names* were accurate. In 1864 you would have found any hamlet called Shady Grove looking about as advertised, with its dappled sunshine filtering through a picturesque grove of cottonwood.

Also at Shady Grove, you would have likely found one or two of Gen. Hancock's soldiers to be *wearing* shades.

Sunglasses, which had a bottle-blue film covering their oval lenses, were similar to the regular eyeglasses worn by older Civil War troops. In turn, these were similar to the replica and antique nineteenth-century frames available from a Baltimore business named Spectacle Accoutrements. The firm offers eyeglasses of gold, brass, silver, steel, and silver plate with either curved or straight temple endpieces; and a 14-karat gold pince-nez pair (upon which Spectacle Accoutrements has grandly bestowed the title *Prince*-Nez). The company also offers versions of early- and late-nineteenth-century eyeglass frames. All require presentation of a current prescription or a pair of specs bearing the owner's lenses.

Prices: Straight end-piece spectacle frames in steel, $55; in brass or silverplate, $65. Curved end-piece spectacles in gold, $85; in brass, $75; in silver, $65. Pince-nez Franklin spectacles in 14-karat gold, $85. Cases included. Add $5 to cover the cost of shipping and handling.

Free illustrated price sheet available.

Spectacle Accoutrements
2918 North Rolling Road
Baltimore, MD 21244
Phone: 410-281-6069

Similar goods available from:

The Grand Spectacle
528 West Water Street
Elmira, New York 14905
Phone: 607-732-7500
Free brochure.

Pitcher & Basin

Although the acquaintance that many soldiers had with personal hygiene was a nodding one, others yearned for cleanliness as an antidote to the filth, body lice, and overall deprivation of war. Here, the wishes of soldiers as different as the Alabama officer who looked forward to when he could "put on a white shirt and… feel for a little while like a white man again" echoed those of the Connecticut sergeant who, during the union siege of Port Hudson, wanted to "go off somewhere and have a good cry, put on some clean clothes, get a letter from home, that I would be ready to come back and die like a Christian."

To relieve such torment, soldiers had such interim means available to them as represented by Village Tinsmithing's pitcher and round camp basin. The former has a 2½ quart capacity, while the latter measures 12 inches in diameter around its wired rim, and 5 inches deep.

Price: $53

Soap tin, copper soap box, and match safe tin also available.

Catalog specializing in period tinware obtainable.

The Village Tinsmithing Works
P.O. Box 189
Randolph, OH 44265
Phone: 330-325-9101

A photographer's wagon

At the beginning of hostilities, photographers such as Mathew Brady and Alexander Gardner applied their twenty-two-year-old craft to the task of portraying war. This required hauling their cumbersome wet-plate cameras off into the field in special wagons. Within the darkened confines of these vehicles, assistants removed 8-by-10-inch glass plates from dust-proof boxes and sensitized them before rushing them out to the camera for exposure. After the photographer tripped the shutter, the assistant would hasten the plate back into the wagon and develop it.

Photo by Claude Andre Levet

The peculiar stiffness often seen among subjects in Civil War photographs is due to the inability of a mid-century lens to freeze a horse's tossing head, much less the clash of armies. While this limitation didn't much interfere with portrait photography, clear depictions of camp and field life required static subjects. Moreover, as these were often rural folk, and always Victorians, they were likely even more sobered by their momentous participation in the new technology. American soldiers being what they are, however, many Civil War photographs reveal the same relaxed camaraderie as found among the troops' twentieth-century counterparts.

Claude Andre Levet's work resembles nothing so much as an undiscovered cache of original Civil War photographs. Using original equipment and such nineteenth-century photographic techniques as "wet collodion" (a method employed from 1850 to 1875 using a solution of nitrated cellulose in a mixture of alcohol and ether). Mr. Levet produces ambrotypes, tintypes and glass negatives. In addition to the Civil War art prints he has available by mail, Levet is available for lectures, demonstrations, and instruction in nineteenth-century photographic processes.

Self-portrait by Claude Andre Levet

Neither blue nor gray in mood, soldiers "skylark" for a Confederate cameraman just before First Bull Run.

Prices: Ambrotypes (glass negatives backed by dark surfaces making them appear positive), $35 to $75; tintypes (positives taken directly on thin metal plates), $30 to $50; prints, $15 to $40.

Catalog available, $2.

The Silver Sunbeam Photographic Gallery
Claude Andre Levet, Collodion Artist
P.O. Box 269
Reserve, LA 70084
Phone: 504-535-8629

FIELD

"*It must be borne in mind that war on a scale inaugurated by this rebellion was decidedly new to us, if not the civilized world.*"

—Union Major General
Rufus Ingalls

"*Give them hell! Give them solid shot! Damn them, give them anything.*"

—Capt. James E. Smith
4th New York Battery

ARTILLERY BARRELS

Owing to a lack of raw materials and skilled munitions workers, the Confederacy had a problem supplying heavy ordnance. This was partly overcome through Southern ability to build arsenals, foundries, and munitions plants to supplant Richmond's famous Tredegar Works. Even so, Confederate troops sometimes had to shape logs as cannon in an attempt to deceive the enemy. These "Quaker guns" (black-painted versions of Confederate 6-pounders, and British and captured Union ordnance) were authentic Civil War fakery. The following replicas are imposters of a different sort. And while they are fully functioning artillery, they are more likely to be trained on the sensibilities of milling tourists than the ranks of advancing armies.

During the war, Northern field artillery consisted mostly of smoothbore Napoleons and the Parrott cast-iron 10-pounder, both of which were muzzle-loaders. Owing to its superiority, the Parrott became the standard Union field piece as the conflict progressed. Added to this were heavier guns, such as the Parrott 30-pounder, a 4.2-inch rifle.

While for siege artillery, and the defense of permanent fortifications the North used cannon like the 24-pounder siege howitzer, the largest piece of ordnance used by either side was the gargantuan Federal "Dictator." This 8½ ton mortar was used to throw its 220-pound, 13-inch shells with horrific effect during the siege of Petersburg, Virginia.

"Whistling Dick"

Noble Brothers Confederate 6-Pounder Cannon Barrel

The Confederate 6-pounder was chiefly used by the highly mobile horse artillery, which served with cavalry. From an original made at the Noble Brothers works, South Bend Replicas' 6-pounder cannon barrel is 73 inches long, weighs 1,000 lbs. and has a 3-inch bore.

Price: $6,073, firing piece.

Parrott Guns, 10 & 20-Pounders

The range of rifled field guns like the 10-pounder Parrott was about two miles. South Bend's 2.9 inch Parrott has been replicated from original drawings. Length, 78 inches; weight, 890 lbs.; bore, 8 inches, smooth. Specimens appear at Fort Pillow, in Tennessee and at the Louisiana State Military Museum.

Although large rifles were known to have grave defects, the 20-pounder Parrotts were considered among the war's best field pieces. Also produced from drawings of an original, South Bend's 20-pounder Parrott is 89½ inches long, weighs 1,750 lbs., and is a 3⅝-inch smoothbore.

Prices: $5,718 and $9,714 respectively for firing pieces.

Siege Howitzer, 24-Pounder

This gun is a replica of one of forty that unsuccessfully defended Fort Pulaski in "the first combat of rifled guns and masonry forts," on April 11, 1862. From Tybee Island, at a range of one to two miles, Union Gen. Quincy Adams Gillmore used ten rifles and twenty-six smoothbores to breach the fort's 7½-foot-thick walls in a little more than twenty-four hours. South Bend's 24-pounder flank howitzer has been replicated from original drawings and examinations of the original. It is 69 inches long, weighs approximately 1,500 lbs. and has a 5.8-inch bore. A specimen appears at the Fort Pulaski National Monument in Georgia.

Price: $10,892, firing piece.

"Catalog of Antique/Replica Ordnance," $7.

South Bend Replicas, Inc.
61650 Oak Road
South Bend, IN 46614
Phone: 219-289-4500

Similar barrels, including a Model 1857 Napoleon 12-pounder and a Coehorn Mortar 24-pounder, available from:

Steen Cannons
10730 Midland Trail Road
Cannonsburg, KY 41120
Phone & Fax: 606-329-2477

Gatling Gun

From the windows of the *New York Tribune,* two machine guns faced the mob storming through the streets below. Publisher Horace Greeley had received the Gatlings as a promotion, and while the New York Draft Riots raged he used them to discourage any rabble advancing in his direction.

Improving on the technology provided by the 1852 Ager Union gun and the 1856 Barnes Machine Cannon, Dr. Richard Jordan Gatling patented his "revolving gun battery" in November, 1862. Like the discredited Ager, the Gatling used .58-caliber charges fired by a crank-operated action. But unlike the Union gun, the Gatling's six rotating barrels had time to cool during firing, enabling them to discharge faster and for a greater time.

As stated in a letter to President Lincoln, Gatling believed that use of his gun was "just the thing needed to aid in crushing the present rebellion"—but efforts to sell the army on his repeater met with bureaucratic stonewalling. This may have been because the doctor hailed from North Carolina, a circumstance that created some suspicion in U.S. government circles. Gatling nevertheless persisted. On one of his many trips to Washington, the doctor called on Brigadier Gen. J.W. Ripley, Chief of Ordnance, to ask that the weapon be tested, but Ripley flatly refused to consider it. So when a representative of Gatling's approached Gen. Benjamin F. Butler in Baltimore asking to demonstrate the weapon, he was careful to omit word of Ripley's response. It didn't matter though, for "Spoons" Butler (so characterized for allegedly stealing the silver during his occupation of New Orleans) was so enthusiastic about the gun's performance he plunked down a grand of his own for each of twelve Gatlings, and directed their use during the siege of Petersburg, Virginia.

The U.S. Army did not adopt the Gatling gun until 1866, following Lee's surrender. But for generations thereafter, the weapon was used in every major conflict—including the Franco-Prussian and Spanish-American Wars—throughout the world.

George Shimek, a "forge and anvil" blacksmith out of Waterloo, Iowa, became interested in the Gatling gun after he saw one in a 1982 Civil War battle reenactment in East Davenport. Using copies of the original drawing submitted by Gatling for his patent, Shimek began building his reproduction in January, 1983, completing the piece in about 250 hours. Mr. Shimek's .50-caliber Gatling gun is a scale replica of the 1862 model. It will fire 200 rounds per minute, and according to its maker, is highly accurate.

Dimensions: Overall length, 38 inches; barrel length, 2 inches. Weight, 135 lbs. (without carriage).

Price: $10,000. Complete mechanical blueprints, $25.

Custom Blacksmithing and Manufacturing
827 Commercial
Waterloo, IA 50702
Phone: 319-291-2095

Similar goods obtainable from:

Schneider Enterprises
1252 N. Brownslake Road
Burlington, WI 53105-9794
Phone & Fax: 414-534-6813

Artilleryman's Valise

A part of the artilleryman's horse equipments, the artillery valise was distinguished by its extra straps. All were made of thick bridle leather, and had round leather handles at each end.

Artillery gunner's haversack, tube pouch, belt, and driver's leg guard also obtainable.

Catalog of cavalry horse and military equipments, $3.

F. Burgess & Company
200 Pine Place
Red Bank, NJ 07701
Phone: 908-576-1624

Gunner's Haversack

Haversacks were used with field pieces and mortars to prevent accidents while the cartridges were being carried to the guns. Made of russet bag leather, the gunner's haversack was to have its front and back connected by gussets which formed the ends and bottoms, allowing the back to be folded flat. The Cavalry Shop's version is also available in black and can be embossed "US or "CS."

Price: $78.

Civil War leather goods catalog available.

The Cavalry Shop
9700 Royerton Drive
Richmond, VA 23228
Phone: 804-266-0898

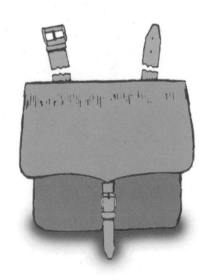

REVOLVERS

Val Forgett founded the Navy Arms company in 1958 after his experience with the North-South Skirmish Association triggered his awareness of the need for well-replicated historic firearms. All of Navy Arms' guns are shooting pieces, safer by far than their "guess and by God" antecedents.

The word "navy" was used to identify U.S. military firearms centuries before the Navy company's Edsel-era birth. The earliest citation appears in a 1777 description of battle by an officer in the Continental Navy. Later, the word was most often applied to a single revolver—the .36-caliber 1851 Colt.

U.S. 1860 Army Revolver (.44 Caliber)

This gun was the standard U.S. sidearm issued during the Civil War. The Springfield Armory Museum in Springfield, Massachusetts reports that the Federal government bought 129,730 of the revolvers, paying $17.69 each. Some 1860 armies were issued with a detachable shoulder stock, but they were unpopular with the troops and soon "lost" by soldiers

Navy Arms' replica has a blued barrel and roll-engraved cylinder, a brass trigger guard, steel backstrap, and case-hardened frame.

Dimensions: Overall length, 13 inches; barrel length, 7½ inches. Weight: 2 lbs. 12 oz.

Price: Finished piece: $175.

Navy Arms Company
689 Bergen Boulevard
Ridgefield, NJ 07657
Phone: 201-945-2500
Fax: 201-945-6859
Order Desk: 800-669-NAVY

C.S. Model 1860 "Reb" Revolver (.36 or .44 Caliber)

I need it bad.

— Sixteen-year-old Confederate Pvt. Henry Pippitt in a letter to his mother asking her to buy him the "Reb" revolver.

At the commencement of the Civil War, the agricultural South faced difficulties in procuring arms for the fight. Other than the old flintlock and percussion rifle muskets that volunteers brought from home, the fledgling Confederacy had to rely on captured weapons and the perpetually insufficient output of its arms manufacturers. Principal among these was the Georgia firm of Griswold and Gunnison. Under contract to the C.S. from 1862 to 1864, the company produced the Model 1860 percussion revolver, which is basically a copy of the 1851 Navy.

Despite the example of Pvt. Pippitt, both Union and Confederate soldiers found revolvers to be an unnecessary burden, the latter often sending them home for use as protection against ruffians, runaways, shirkers, and blue-coat invaders.

Navy Arms' replica of the Model 1860 features a brass frame and backstrap with blued barrel and cylinder. The hammer, loading lever, and trigger are case-hardened. The revolver is also available in kit form.

Dimensions: Overall length, 13 inches; barrel length, 7½ inches. Weight: 2 lbs. 12 oz.

Prices: Finished .36-caliber piece, $115; finished .44-caliber piece, $115.

LeMat Revolvers

This firearm was patented in 1856 by Dr. Jean Alexander Francois LeMat of New Orleans and perfected with the help of General P.G.T. Beauregard. It became the favored sidearm of J.E.B. Stuart and many other secessionist navy, cavalry, and infantry officers.

The LeMats may be considered tangible evidence of Europe's Confederate sympathies. Produced in shops in and around Paris, the revolvers were completed in Birmingham, England and sent on to Bermuda to be loaded onto blockade runners for final shipment into the C.S. The nine-shot revolver with its lower, single-shot barrel of approximately .60 caliber (hence its nickname, the "grapeshot pistol"), gave Confederate combatants a deadly advantage in the field.

The Navy Arms' LeMat has all-steel construction with a polished blue finish. Its hammer and trigger are color case-hardened. The walnut stock is hand-checkered and oil finished. In addition to the LeMat Mould, an "exact copy of the original" in solid brass and case-hardened steel, Navy Arms offers distinct Army, Navy, and Cavalry Models. In addition, their 18th Georgia LeMat is based on the Navy model and bears the legend "*Deo Vindice*"; while the Beauregard LeMat is a replica of the one carried by the splendid-looking "Hero of Sumter" and which is now on display at the Museum of the Confederacy in Richmond.

Dimensions: Overall length, 14 inches; barrel length, 7⅝ inches. Weight: 3 lbs., 7 oz.

Price: Finished piece, $595.

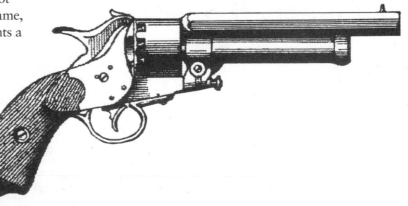

C.S. Spiller & Burr Revolver (.36 Caliber)

This percussion revolver was one of many Confederate Colt knockoffs. It was first produced for the South by Spiller & Burr of Atlanta between 1862 and 1864. After the company was unable to comply with an order for 15,000 pieces, the Confederate government bought it and moved it to the Macon (Georgia) Armory.

Navy Arms' replica comes with brass frame, reiffe guard, backstrap and top strap. It has an octagonal blued barrel and cylinder.

Dimensions: Overall length, 12½ inches; barrel length, 7 inches. Weight: 2 lbs. 8 oz.

Price: Finished piece, $145.

Catalog of replica firearms and accessories, $2.

Navy Arms Company
689 Bergen Boulevard
Ridgefield, NJ 07657
Phone: 201-945-2500
Fax: 201-945-6859
Order Desk: 800-669-NAVY

C. S. Schneider & Glassik Brass Frame Revolver (.36 Caliber)

These brass-framed copies of the 1851 Colt were produced for the C.S. by the Memphis, Tennessee, firm of Schneider and Glassik, about which little else is known. Production of the revolvers ceased with the 1862 fall of Memphis, and the few examples remaining testify to their hard use in the Trans-Mississippi.

Euroarms' replica Schneider & Glassik Colt is of "traditional Southern design," according to its current manufacturer, with a rifled, octagonal barrel of 7 inches and overall length of 13 inches. The rear sight is a "V" notch, groove in hammer. A truncated-cone front-sight is made of brass, as are the weapon's frame, trigger guard, and backstrap. Grips are of finished walnut. Weight: 40-ounces.

Dimensions:
Overall length, 13 inches; barrel length, 7½ inches. Weight: 40 ounces.

Recommended ball diameter: .375 round or conical, pure lead.

Price: $120.

U.S. Rogers & Spencer Army Revolver (.44 Caliber)

The Utica, New York, firm of Rogers & Spencer produced 5,000 of the .44-caliber revolvers under contract to the U.S. government in the final year of the war. According to its present manufacturer, many authorities consider this design to be the best of the percussion era.

Dimensions: Overall length, 13¾ inches; barrel length, 7½ inches. Weight: 47 ounces. Recommended ball diameter, .451 round or conical, of pure lead. Flared, finished-walnut grips.

Price: $227.

Brochure, price, and retailer lists available.

Euroarms of America
P.O. Box 3277
Winchester, VA 22604
Phone: 540-662-1863
Fax: 540-662-4464

1851 & 1861 Navy Revolvers (.36 Caliber)

The Model 1851 Navy was one of the most popular sidearms of the Civil War. Unlike the 1860 Army (with which it shared this distinction) the 1851 Navy was favored by the South and spawned many Confederate copies. The piece was manufactured until 1876 (Wild Bill Hickok always carried a pair). By comparison, the 1861 Navy sold barely more than 2,000 pieces, its popularity limited by the continuing appeal of the 1851 model, and a disastrous fire at the Colt factory in 1864. Both revolvers are six-shooters with engraved barrels, have forged steel barrels, color case-hardened frames and walnut grips. The 1861 favors forged steel over the 1851's brass as the metal for its backstrap and trigger guard.

Specifications: Overall length, 13 inches; barrel length, 7½ inches; weight, 2¾ lbs.

Price: 1851 Navy, $270; 1861 Navy, $295.

Color catalog of replica nineteenth-century rifles and revolvers available.

Uberti USA Inc.
P.O. Box 469
Lakeville, CT 06039
Phone: 860-435-8068 & 860-435-2846
Fax: 860-435-8146
E-mail: uberti@li.com

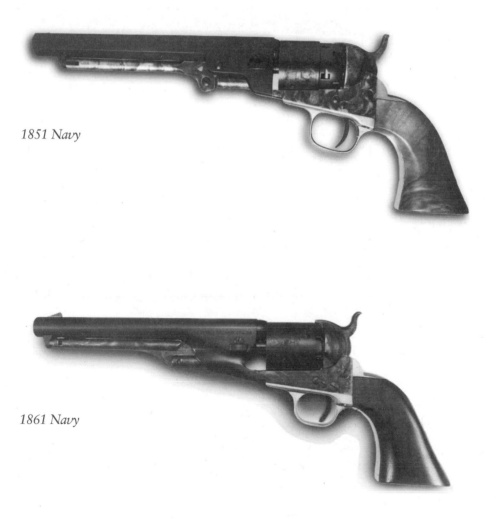

1851 Navy

1861 Navy

RIFLES

1841 Mississippi Rifle (.54 & .58 Caliber)

The Old Mississippi Rifle, carrying a half-ounce ball, is a favorite with them.

— Rodney Glisan, *Journal of Army Life*, 1874.

The Mississippi rifle was called the "United States Rifle" until 1847 when Jefferson Davis' Mississippi Regiment used it to turn back Santa Anna at the decisive battle of Buena Vista.

Although it was obsolete by 1855, the percussion-lock gun's reputation caused the Colt company to re-bore it to accommodate the Union Army's .58 caliber minié-ball in 1861.

Dimensions: Overall length, 48 inches; barrel length, 33 inches. Weight: 9 lbs, 8 oz.

Price: Finished piece, $465.

1853 Enfield Three-Band Musket (.58 Caliber)

Our equipments, I understand are all ready. We are to be armed with the long ranged Enfield rifles. I conclude, hoping by and by to give you something interesting from 'Dixie.'

—From the Correspondence of Pvt. Charles Moulton of the 34th Vol. Massachusetts Infantry to the Berkshire (Mass.) Eagle, 1862.

The .58-caliber Enfield Model 1853 was originally built at the London Armory Company in Enfield, England, for use by the British admiralty. Considered to be one of the best imported arms to see service during the war, the three-band musket was purchased in large amounts by both the U.S. and C.S. governments. Versions were made in Windsor, Vermont under license from Her Majesty's government exclusively for the North.

Similar to the Springfield Rifle (the machine tools at the Enfield armory were direct copies of those at the U.S. Armory at Springfield, Massachusetts), the Enfield was admired in one contemporary account as "a beautiful arm [that] presented a natty appearance." Navy Arms' replica features a case-hardened lock, a cold-forged steel barrel, and a walnut stock with brass furniture.

Dimensions: Overall length, 55 inches; barrel length, 39 inches. Weight: 9 lbs., 9 oz.

Price: Finished piece, $480.

Catalog of replica firearms and accessories, $2.

1859 "Berdan" Sharps Rifle (.54 Caliber)

A single-shot, breech-loading sniper rifle used by Col. Hiram Berdan and the green-jacketed 1st and 2nd U.S. Sharpshooters Regiments. Claiming to have eliminated more Confederate soldiers than any other force of comparable size, Berdan's men were proud of their powerful rifles' ability to silence rebel batteries.

The Navy replica features double-set triggers and color case-hardened furniture.

Dimensions: Overall length, 46³/₄ inches; barrel length, 30 inches. Weight: 8 lbs., 8 oz.

Price: Finished piece, $1095.

U.S. Military Henry (.44 Caliber)

The Henry repeater made its debut in 1862. By dint of massive firepower, the military model was considered the Civil War's most effective rifle. The Henry was widely used by Union soldiers as the South lacked the industrial capacity to produce one like it. Consistent with the original, the Navy Arms replica has sling swivels mounted on the left side and a

buttplate with a trap.

Dimensions: Overall length, 43 inches; barrel length, 24 inches. Weight: 9 lbs., 4 oz.

Price: Finished piece, $895.

1863 C.S. Richmond Musket (.58 Caliber)

Utilizing 1855 rifle musket parts taken from the Harper's Ferry Arsenal in 1861, the Confederacy manufactured this long arm at the Richmond Armory. Similar in design to the 1861 Springfield, the Richmond Musket used a different rear sight, brass buttplate and forend cap. The 1855-style "hump-

back" lockplate is marked "1863 C.S. Richmond VA."

Dimensions: Overall length, 56 inches; barrel length, 40 inches. Weight: 10 lbs., 4 oz.

Price: Finished piece, $550.

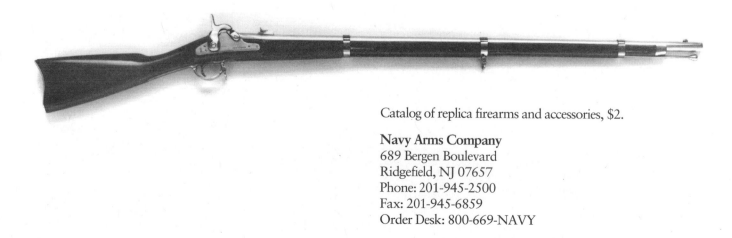

Catalog of replica firearms and accessories, $2.

Navy Arms Company
689 Bergen Boulevard
Ridgefield, NJ 07657
Phone: 201-945-2500
Fax: 201-945-6859
Order Desk: 800-669-NAVY

U.K. London Armory Company Enfield Musketoon P-1861 (.58 Caliber)

The P-1861 Enfield Musketoon is the carbine version of the P-1853 Enfield Rifle-Musket. Developed by the British in response to the needs of artillery crews for a short, accurate weapon, the Enfield musketoon was widely used on both sides during the Civil War.

Euroarms' replica of the London Armory Company's Enfield Musketoon has a color case-hardened lock that is stamped with both the V.R. (Victoria Regina) crown and the manufacturer's mark. It features a blued barrel with a removable breech-plug, and a buttplate and trigger guard made from solid-cast and polished brass.

Specifications: Barrel length, 24 inches; overall length, 40½ inches; weight 7 pounds 7½ ounces (varies with density of wood). Use black powder only.

Price: $427.

C.S. Cook & Brother Artillery Carbine (.58 Caliber)

The firm of Cook & Brother, owned and operated by Ferdinand W.C. and Francis T. Cook, had been successfully established in New Orleans long before the Civil War. With the outbreak of hostilities in 1861, the brothers offered their services to the Confederate government and were soon turning out arms for Alabama and possibly Louisiana. The Cook & Brother armory employed nearly 400 workers and produced approximately 600 guns per month by the end of the year.

The fall of New Orleans to the Union fleet of Adm. David Farragut in April, '62 required evacuation of the factory to Athens, Georgia—an area then safe from enemy action. By early in '63, a new two-story building of brick and stone was again producing arms bearing the Cook & Brother name, their lockplates stamped with a Confederate flag. The firm's supply of greatly needed arms peaked in late '63, with approximately 750 guns of all models produced per month.

Sherman's 1864 invasion of Georgia required that the armory work force be organized into a battalion attached to the local militia, with Ferdinand Cook as major and his brother as captain. With the fall of Atlanta, the production of arms was halt-ed when the battalion was called up. Maj. Cook was killed in December '64, and the firm of Cook & Brother died with the Confederacy.

Euroarms' replica of the 1861 New Orleans Cook & Brother Artillery Carbine has a color case-hardened lock that is stamped with the image of the Confederate flag and the legend "Cook & Brother N.O. 1861." It features a walnut stock; a rifled barrel with a removable breech screw, per the original; and barrel bands, sling swivels, a buttplate, nosecap, and trigger guard of polished brass.

Specifications: Barrel length, 24 inches; overall length, 40⅓ inches; weight 7-pounds 7½ ounces (varies with density of wood). Black powder only.

Price: $470.

Brochure, price, and retailer lists available.

Euroarms of America
P.O. Box 3277
Winchester, VA 22604
Phone: 540-662-1863
Fax: 540-662-4464

Soldiers of a New York Zouave regiment.

Zouave Rifle (.58 Caliber)

Many regiments of both the Union and Confederate armies modeled themselves on the French colonial Zouaves, soldiers famous for their ability to load and fire from a prone position. Nonetheless, aping the Zouaves was predominantly a sartorial matter that involved the wholesale adoption of their brightly colored uniforms—including the baggy trousers; the short jackets; and the gaudy turbans or fezzes that might be found in a Masonic Lodge's production of *Sinbad the Sailor*. Lest you think this 1800s Algerian light infantry uniform would appear somehow less ridiculous on the back of a nineteenth-century American soldier, I refer you to Union Gen. John W. Phelps who, upon encountering his first Zouave—a declared officer—roared: "An officer! I thought you were a circus clown!"

Dimensions: Overall length, 49 inches; barrel length, 33 inches. Weight: 9-pounds; recommended bullet, .58-caliber minié.

Price: Finished piece, $465.

Navy Arms Company
689 Bergen Boulevard
Ridgefield, NJ 07657
Phone: 201-945-2500
Fax: 201-945-6859
Order Desk: 800-669-NAVY

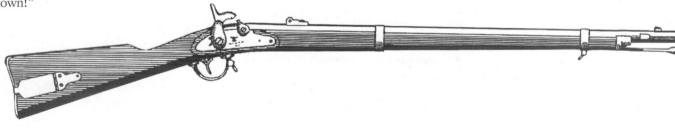

AMMUNITION

Cartridges

The variety of small arms used during the war was reflected in the many calibers they required, complicating the problem of supply. One ordnance expert noted that Civil War calibers generally ranged from .40 to .61 (the caliber of a bullet or shell is its diameter measured in inches) and that 20 different calibers of ammunition, from .44 to .69, had been furnished for a single expedition. "In 1861," he continued, "when every tyro [recruit] knew that a breech-loader was best … the Chief of Ordnance had stated that 'a Harper's Ferry smooth bore muzzle-loading gun, with buck and ball, was the best arm that could be placed in the hands of a soldier,' and asserted that he would have no such gun as a breech-loader in service because 'it would require a mule to carry the ammunition for each soldier.'"

Cartridges Unlimited of St. Louis supplies rolled paper cartridges in the .44 (Remington) to .69 (Springfield) caliber range. Differing cartridges are available as live ammunition, as blanks, or as dummies filled with railroad ballast. Cast bullets, ranging in caliber from .44 to .58, are also obtainable.

Prices: Live cartridges for Springfield .58 caliber and Sharp's Carbine .52 and .54 caliber, $9.50 per box of ten. For British Enfield .577 caliber and Sharp's .52 and .54 caliber (combustible), $10 per box of ten. Price for a box of six Remington .44 caliber live cartridges, $6.50.

Ammunition Pack Labels

Paper, foil, or sheepskin cartridges were issued from arsenals in packs of six. These labels come five for a dollar.

Free price list of cartridges, ammunition boxes, labels, and souvenirs available.

Cartridges Unlimited
4320-A Hartford Street
St. Louis, MO 63116
Phone: 314-664-4332

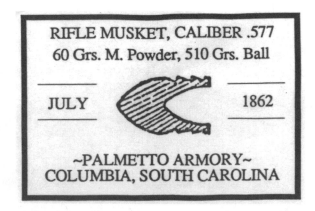

Ammunition Boxes

Ammo boxes were simple affairs usually made of dovetailed white pine boards, finished and nailed together. Wooden handles were nailed to both ends and six screws fastened the lid, under which the place and date of the manufacture of the cartridges inside was indicated. Box color also indicated the kind of cartridges within, and both their type and number was marked on each end. An ammunition box shown in *The Civil War Collector's Encyclopedia* bears the legend: "609 BALL CARTG COLTS NAVY BELT PISTOL 1864."

The House of Kirk's ammunition boxes are built with the proper box joint corners. The Union model is painted, while the C.S. version is not, per originals. An oil finish protects the wood.

Dimensions: Union and Confederate ammunition boxes, 16 inches wide by 11 inches long by 8 inches deep.

Price: $65 each.

Price sheet for Civil War replica writing box, stamps, stationery and ammunition boxes available.

House of Kirk
9380 Collins Parkway
P.O. Box 808
New Market, VA 22844
Phone: 540-740-8296
Fax: 540-740-4459

EDGED WEAPONS

SWORDS & SABERS

In addition to their evident usefulness as weapons, sabers and swords were salient aspects of the proper martial presentation. They were always to be worn while on duty, and be replaced by swords of honor (or the prescribed sword in a gilt scabbard) while off. That Civil War swords pointed to a soldier's rank and branch of service is demonstrated by their great variety, a significant portion of which is replicated by Legendary Arms of Dunellen, New Jersey.

Catalog available.

Legendary Arms, Inc.
P.O. Box 29
Dunellen, NJ 08812-0299
Phone: 908-424-8636
Fax: 908-424-2303
Order Line: 800-528-2767

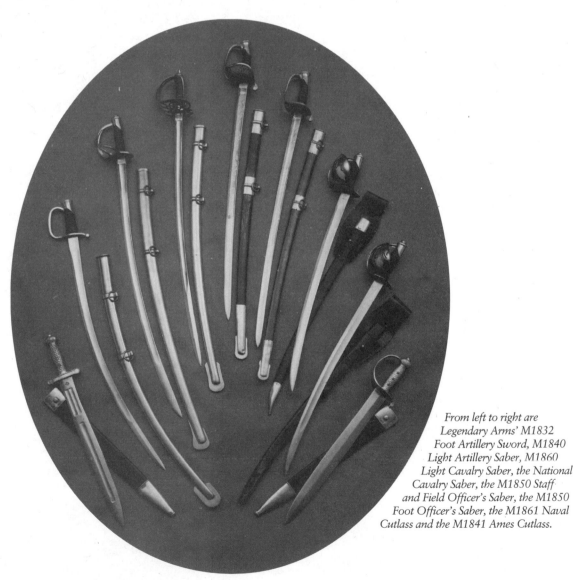

From left to right are Legendary Arms' M1832 Foot Artillery Sword, M1840 Light Artillery Saber, M1860 Light Cavalry Saber, the National Cavalry Saber, the M1850 Staff and Field Officer's Saber, the M1850 Foot Officer's Saber, the M1861 Naval Cutlass and the M1841 Ames Cutlass.

Zouave Bayonet

"This [bayonet] drill was a Frency affair," said one Civil War officer in a telling comment about wartime regard for the practice, "with its *parry, prime, 'se-conde,' tierce, high quarte, lunge, blow with the butt*—all of which kept the men jumping around like so many animated frogs … Perhaps they fight on these scientific principles in France, but in our war nobody ever heard any of these commands given in battle."

"Frency" as well is the Zouave bayonet, a replica *"arme blanche"* with a brass handle, steel blade, and scabbard trimmed in brass as is the original.

Price: $60.

Springfield Bayonet

All U.S. regulation rifles and muskets accepted socket bayonets like this Springfield model. Described as "a savage-looking thing" with its three fluted sides coming to a needle-sharp point, bayonets such as the Springfield are shown by army records to have inflicted few wounds in battle. This may be attributable to the powerful psychological effect of a bayonet charge, in which (like cats with bared claws) one side or the other usually broke before the weapons could do their grisly work. Displaced as an eviscerating weapon of war, bayonets were often used as the household appliances of same—useful for grinding coffee beans in tin cups and, when driven into the ground, as tent pins or candlesticks.

Price: $55. An Enfield rifle bayonet is also available at this price.

Zouave soldiers with bayonets.

Catalog of replica firearms and accessories, $2.

Navy Arms Company
689 Bergen Boulevard
Ridgefield, NJ 07657
Phone: 201-945-2500
Fax: 201-945-6859
Orders: 800-669-NAVY

Confederate D-Guard Bowie

Bowie knives in various lengths and patterns were more popular among Southern troops who couldn't rely on adequate C.S. government issue. The Legendary Arms D-Guard bowie is a replica of the knife carried by a Virginia infantryman. Consistent with the original, the 15½ inch knife has a massive, polished blade 11½ inches long and just over 2 inches wide at the hilt. It comes with a belt-looped, black leather scabbard that has a reinforced throat and tip.

Catalog available.

Price $124.99.

Ames-Dahlgren Knife

Designed circa 1856, by Adm. John A. Dahlgren, about 1,800 of these knives were produced by the Ames Manufacturing Company between 1861 and '64. Made to fit the Whitney Plymouth Navy Rifle, the knives doubled as saber bayonets.

Legendary Arms' Ames-Dahlgren knife comes complete with scabbard.

Price: $124.99.

Legendary Arms, Inc.
P.O. Box 29
Dunellen, NJ 08812-0299
Phone: 908-424-8636
Fax: 908-424-2303
Order Line: 800-528-2767

FEDERAL ARMY UNIFORMS

The Grand Illusions Clothing Company claims to have sold replica Civil War uniforms to customers on nearly every continent. The image this brings to mind is one of a troop of Japanese Johnny Rebs marching into some Asian approximation of Appomattox costumed in Grand Illusions mufti. Nor does the imagination stop there, for American Civil War reenactments of one kind or another can take place from the Hormuz Straits to the Russian Steppes—neither far from recent civil wars and their civilian Andersonvilles.

However it is history—and living history in particular—that is Grand Illusions' undisputed territory. In addition to the world's reenactor markets, the company's "meticulously researched" Civil War uniforms have been made for museums; for the U.S. and state governments; and for such films as "Gettysburg," "Last Confederate Widow," and "Glory" among many others.

New York, Connecticut, and Ohio among other states had their own uniform regulations for troops. The buttons of these militias were designed to give prominence to the state coat of arms, while the remaining bright work—belt buckles and cartridge box plates—ostentatiously featured the letter and figure symbols for which the units were often well known. However, the vast majority of Federal troops were outfitted in accordance with Army Regulations 1861 (Sections 1442-1635), that Grand Illusions follows. The Delaware company's uniforms are copied from artifacts existing in either private or museum collections, with the resulting patterns drafted in-house. (This practice tends to eliminate the ill-advised replication of "shoddies," or the early-war U.S. uniforms made of wool scraps that fell apart in the rain, barely making it as far as First Bull Run.) This allows them such typical nineteenth-century features as "bird breast" lapels, shoulder seams that are dropped at the armhole and angle off in the back, and sleeves that curve at the elbow so as to appear to offer a handshake. Fabrics are wool, linen, cotton, silk and natural blends; and buttons are bone, porcelain, glass, mother-of-pearl, fabric-cover, pewter, brass, and tin.

Enlisted Man's Frock Coat

Between 1860 and 1865 the number of sewing machines used by the U.S. garment industry doubled, in part, to produce the frock coats that were standard issue for all infantry, heavy artillery, and engineer corps. Grand Illusions' version is tailored in dark blue with a cotton half-lining. In accordance with regulations, the coat has a stand-up collar and curve cut sleeves leading to split cuffs. The nine brass eagle buttons on the breast are matched by two others, equidistant at the waist in back, and two on each cuff. Specify collar and cuff piping: sky blue piping for infantry, red for artillery, yellow for engineers, maroon for ordnance, and crimson for hospital stewards.

Price: Sizes 38 through 50, $179.

Staff or Field-Grade Double-Breasted Frock Coat

Grand Illusions' replicas of these coats, which were worn by officers above the rank of captain, have the curved, nineteenth-century "bird's breast" lapels. The coats have small stand-up collars, a single interior breast pocket, curved 1800s sleeves, and sport 14 staff eagle buttons arrayed on the breast, four on the back, and three on each sleeve. Major General's coats were to have two rows of buttons on the chest with nine in each row, placed by threes. This and other officers' button spacing patterns, as well as velvet collars and cuffs, are available on request.

Prices: Sizes 38 through 50: field and staff grade, $199. General's grade, $218.

Company or Junior Officer's Frock Coat

Army Regulations of 1861 specified that a junior (or company) officer's coat be distinguished by its being single- rather than double-breasted. Grand Illusions' junior officer's frock coat is copied from one worn by Gideon B. Todd of the 2nd Delaware Infantry. In addition to its single-breast, it has the correct stand-up collar, curved sleeves, interior breast pocket, and brass eagle buttons. It is made from 16-ounce dark blue wool and completely lined in cotton.

Price: Sizes 38 through 50, $172.

U.S. Roundabout or Shell Jacket

First adopted early in the nineteenth century for use by enlisted men, this dark blue "short jacket" was commonly worn with a kepi by Civil War officers and volunteers as their service uniform. Grand Illusions' fully lined roundabouts are made of wool and have a nine-button breast with a single interior pocket. They are available with or without epaulets and piping.

Prices: Sizes 38 through 50, $89. Double-breasted, $145.

Mounted Uniform Jacket

Used by enlisted men in the cavalry and artillery, these dark blue woolen jackets are trimmed with braids of yellow for the former and red for the latter. The waist-length garments curve down to points in the front and back, where two small belts "pillow-in" the back seams. Also, the dashing jackets feature a tall standing collar with two small eagle buttons on each side, and two others on each split cuff. Twelve small eagle buttons run down the breast.

Price: Sizes 38 through 50, $139.

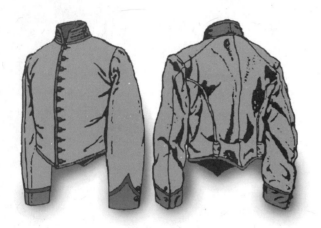

Officer's Greatcoat

According to Regulations, "cloak coat" of dark blue cloth, Grand Illusions' officer's greatcoat is of heavyweight wool, half-lined in wool or cotton sleeve-lining, with two pockets set outside. Black braids on the sleeves were used to indicate rank as follows: Generals, five braids with a double knot; colonels, five braids with a single knot; lieutenant colonels, four braids with a single knot, majors, three braids with a single knot; captains, two braids with a single knot; 1st lieutenants, one braid with a single knot.

Price: Small sizes 38 to 40, medium sizes 42 to 44, large sizes 46 to 48, and extra-large sizes 50 to 52. $235.

Mounted Pattern Greatcoat

A double-breasted, caped overcoat made from heavy sky blue wool. The wrist-length cape is longer than the elbow-length version on the foot greatcoat (also available) and has 12 small eagle buttons along the placket. The coat is half-lined in wool and has turn-down cuffs and a stand-and-fall collar. Regulations specified the buttons to be the same as used by the artillery, omitting the letter in the shield.

Price: Small sizes 38 to 40, medium sizes 42 to 44, large sizes 46 to 48, and extra-large sizes 50 to 52. $198.

Sack Coat/Fatigue Blouse

This oft-encountered coat of dark blue flannel was initially intended for use as fatigue dress exclusively, but shortages caused it to be employed for field use. The coat was commonly referred to as the "four buttons." Grand Illusions' 12-ounce woolen coat has four brass eagle buttons and a turn-down collar. The relatively lightweight blouses are unlined, as per original government issue.

Price: Sizes 36 through 50, $59. With optional lining, $74.

Military Vest

Vests such as these were widely used on both sides of the war. As nonregulation items, the vests were privately made by tailors or family members. Grand Illusions' vests are copied from one worn by a Delaware officer killed in 1864. It has three external welt pockets in front, nine small buttons, and a belted back with buckle. The vest is available in sky blue, dark blue, cream, gray, and butternut.

Price: Sizes 38 through 50, $48.

Invalid Corps Coat

The Invalid Corps was established in April 1863 for officers and men of the Union army who, due to injury or illness were deemed unfit for combat duty. On March 18, 1864 this name was changed to the Veteran Reserve Corps to relieve it of having to share initials with the "Inspected—Condemned" code that the army stamped on all worn-out animals and equipment. The association was just too humiliatingly close.

It was these men, in their sky blue invalid coats, who were largely guarding Washington, D.C. when Confederate Gen. Jubal Anderson Early began his July 1864 raid there. Officers wore regulation kepis, sky blue frock coats with dark blue rank bars, and sky blue trousers with two dark blue stripes down the seam. Other ranks had kepis and trousers like the regular army, worn with "sky blue jersey jackets cut along the waist." The distinction made by the invalid corps' jackets and coats made them extremely unpopular, and they were eventually replaced with normal dark blue frock coats.

Grand Illusions' Invalid Corps roundabout coat is split at the sides and cuffs and is trimmed with dark blue tape around the edges, epaulets, collar, and cuffs. Eleven small brass eagle buttons close the front.

Price: Sizes 38 through 50, $139.

Foot Pattern Trousers

"Foot" as in non-mounted infantry, these trousers are full-cut with a gusset in the crotch for grunt use. They are available in sky or dark blue (General Order 108, Headquarters of the Army, December 16, 1861, authorized sky blue as the color. Few enlisted men wore dark blue trousers) with fly buttons of pewter or cast tin. Grand Illusions' trousers also come with suspender buttons, a back adjustment tie, and choice of side seam or mule-ear pockets.

Price: Sizes 30 through 44, $68 (add $15 for the mule-ear pockets).

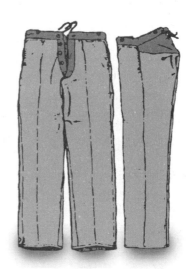

Noncommissioned Officer's Trousers

These are foot or mounted trousers bearing 1-inch service stripes for sergeants, 1/2 inch for corporals. Once again, branch colors are: infantry, blue; heavy artillery, red; engineers and cavalry yellow.

Prices: Sizes 30 to 44, $78 for foot N.C.O.s, $88 for mounted.

Catalog available, $4.

Grand Illusions Clothing Company
705 Interchange Boulevard
Newark, DE 19711
Phone: 302-366-0300
Fax: 302-738-1858

Mounted Pattern Army Trousers

These were issued to mounted artillerymen and officers as well as cavalrymen. Grand Illusions' issue are made of seat-reinforced heavy wool and have back yokes, back waist adjustments, and high waistbands. Choose mule-ear or side-seam pockets, pewter or tin suspender buttons.

Price: Sizes 30 through 44, $79 (add $15 for mule-ear pockets).

Officer's Trousers

These are available in foot or mounted pattern with a $\frac{1}{8}$ inch welt in side seams bearing above service colors or gold for staff officers. Medical cadets would receive these trousers with a welt of buff-colored cloth.

Price: Sizes 30 through 44, $79 for foot officers, $89 for mounted.

Catalog available, $4.

Grand Illusions Clothing Company
705 Interchange Boulevard
Newark, DE 19711
Phone: 302-366-0300
Fax: 302-738-1858

Similar goods obtainable from:

Greta Cunningham
402 East Main Street
Madison, IN 47250
Phone: 812-273-4193

Mrs. Cunningham's Union enlisted frock coats were recommended by *The Watchdog*, a quarterly devoted to furthering the authenticity of Civil War replicas. *The Watchdog* is available for $7 a year by writing P.O. Box 4582, Frankfort, KY 40604-4582.

CONFEDERATE ARMY UNIFORMS

Like the Confederacy's coins, international alliances, march on Harrisburg, and uncontested independence—her uniforms were partly the stuff of dreams. Perhaps that's why soldiers were sometimes half naked in them, and on the run.

Although few troops got to don the resplendent uniforms described in the Confederate Regulations of 1861 and 1862, their absence was greatly made up for by the tailor-made or company-supplied uniforms of volunteer militias, and by butternut duds sewn at home. A third supplier was the U.S. government, as (although southern authorities tried to discourage the practice) Confederate troops regularly stripped enemy soldiers of their shoes, shirts, skivvies, hats, and clothing. Despite (or due to) such deprivations, as Rod Gragg points out in his book, *The Illustrated Confederate Reader,* "no soldiers ever marched with less to encumber them, and none marched faster or held out longer."

Enlisted Man's Frock Coat

Found in infinite variation during the war, Grand Illusions' Confederate enlisted man's frock coat is based on an original worn by a prisoner in Fort Delaware. The body of the coat is a six-piece cut with a short, stand-up collar, about 1¾ inches high. The skirts are cut long and are fully lined with cotton cloth. The original jean cloth coat had ten buttons down the breast with two others set on the waist in the back. Grand Illusions offers this coat with from seven to ten buttons; fully lined in cotton; with one inside pocket.

Prices: Sizes 38 through 50, $179 in wool, $197 in jean cloth.

Double-Breasted Frock Coat

Derived from a cadet gray (a heavy, blue-gray material) coat that once belonged to a cavalry colonel. Both the wartime original and the Grand Illusions model emulating it have trim on collar and cuffs, gold braided sleeves, and are fully lined in cotton. The Grand Illusions frock coat is available in any of their woolens and branch service colors, and has the inevitable inside breast pocket, a curved breast with two seven-button rows, and up to four rows of gold braid, if desired.

Prices: Sizes 38 to 50, $249, in wool, $264 in jean cloth. Braid and trim are extra.

Catalog available, $4.

Grand Illusions Clothing Company
705 Interchange Boulevard
Newark, DE 19711
Phone: 302-366-0300
Fax: 302-738-1858

Regimental Sack Coat

The single-breasted jacket was inspiration for the derisive term "gray jackets," a name that Union troops also bestowed upon the body lice that plagued both armies. From an original in the collection of Richmond's Museum of the Confederacy, Grand Illusions' Confederate sack coat has a three-piece body with curved sleeves, a short, stand-up collar; and a seven-button breast. It has both an inside and an outside pocket.

Prices: Sizes 38 through 50, $79 in wool, $88 in jean cloth.

Military Vest

The epitome of outerwear for the stripped-down Johnnie, vests were popular non-issue garments often obtained from sutlers. Grand Illusions' Confederate vest has a nine-button breast, three pockets and a stand-up collar and buckle back. It is available with cloth, tin, pewter, or brass buttons.

Prices: Sizes 38 through 50, $48 in wool or cotton, $54 in jean cloth.

Wytheville Depot Shell

From an original owned by the family of a soldier who wore it in 1864 and 1865, this shell is made of a heavy gray cloth with nine brass block-"A" buttons on the breast. It sports a white cotton lining, a single pocket and no trim. The collar is of the short, stand-up variety, approximately an inch-and-a-half high; while the sleeves are cut full with a narrow cuff and a six-piece body.

Prices: Sizes 38 through 50, $89 in wool, $110 in jean cloth.

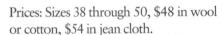

Richmond Depot Shell Jacket

Also known as the Army of Northern Virginia Shell, this was the standard jacket issued to A.N.V. regiments in 1862. It has a short, stand-up collar with a nine-button breast (seven- and eight-button jackets are also known to have been made). The cut of the coat is tight in the armholes with a full sleeve that ends in a narrow 5½ inch cuff. The body of the coat is in six parts, is long waisted and trimmed in piping or tape. The shell is fully lined in cotton and has a single inside breast pocket. Jackets issued in '63 and '64 (Type II) were fitted with epaulets and belt loops; while those issued during the difficult period from mid-1863 through the end of hostilities (Type III) bore neither trim, tape, nor epaulets. Originals of these jackets can be seen at the Museum of the Confederacy and the Smithsonian Institution.

Prices: Type I, in sizes 38 through 50; with belt loops, piping or trim; $115 in wool; $136 in jean cloth. Type II in sizes 38 through 50; with belt loops, epaulets and no trim; $103 in wool; $124 in jean cloth. Type III in sizes 38 through 50; plain; $89 in wool; $110 in jean cloth.

8th Louisiana Shell Jacket

Copied from one worn by Thomas Taylor and now owned by the Museum of the Confederacy, this jacket has an eight-button front, a high stand-up collar that curves down the front, an inside pocket and curved bottom front panels. Fully lined.

Prices: Sizes 38 through 50, $89 in wool, $110 in jean cloth.

Trans-Mississippi Department Shell Jacket

On May 26, 1862, the Confederate Army's Trans-Mississippi Department was created to direct warfare in Texas, Arkansas, Missouri, Western Louisiana, and the Indian territories. Nonetheless, this shell jacket is the match of an original now in a Virginia collection. It is a short-waisted jacket with a six-piece body. It has a seven-button breast, a short stand-up collar and slightly curved bottom front panels. The coat is fully lined and has a large, slanted pocket on its outside left.

Prices: Sizes 38 through 50, $95 wool, $115, jean cloth.

26th North Carolina Shell Jacket

After the coats issued to the men of the 26th North Carolina Infantry, this coat is colored Richmond (dark) gray with French (or purplish) blue piping on its stand-up collar and cuffs. The body is made up of six pieces cut with full-fitted sleeves. It has epaulets and a nine-button breast.

Prices: Sizes 38 through 50, $116 in wool, $146 in jean cloth.

Grand Illusions Clothing Company
705 Interchange Boulevard
Newark, DE 19711
Phone: 302-366-0300
Fax: 302-738-1858

Confederate Double-Breasted Shell Jacket

At about five-foot-nine, James Ewell Brown (or "Jeb") Stuart has been described as "massive and nearly square." He was called "Beauty" Stuart at West Point—a derisive sobriquet the Virginian earned by hiding his chin under a splendid beard. However, the future general's vanity stood in marked contrast to his piety and sincerity—traits not dissimilar from those of his friend, Stonewall Jackson. And as for the chin, it may have been the only thing about Stuart that was not outstanding.

Jeb Stuart was graduated from West Point in 1854 to become seriously wounded by Indians in Kansas during border disturbances there. While on leave, he volunteered to be an aide-de-camp to Lee during John Brown's 1859 raid, following his commander's lead to "go with his state" in '61. The Peninsular campaign found Stuart Captain of C.S.A. Cavalry, marking the beginning of a career of ghostly raids to confound the enemy with deft maneuvers. At Williamsburg in June, '62, Stuart led his troops in his first "ride around McClellan;" and the next month—in an appointment destined to take advantage of his bravery,

endurance, style, and good humor—Stuart took command of the entire A.N.V. Cavalry. He attained this position just before both Second Bull Run and Antietam, where his next ride around Little Mac was accomplished. Stuart led his cavalry division at Fredericksburg and succeeded A.P. Hill as the commander of Jackson's corps at Chancellorsville. Jackson's death at Chancellorsville and Stuart's delay in reaching Lee at Gettysburg were contributing factors to the tide being turned there. On May 11, 1864, he followed Jackson in combat death after being wounded at Yellow Tavern. Lee grieved at Stuart's demise and later said that he could "scarcely think of him without weeping."

Jeb Stuart's Confederate double-breasted shell jacket is now in the collection of the Museum of the Confederacy. "Basically a frock coat without skirts," the Grand Illusions' replica has a standard 14-button front, a solid collar and cuffs, to which braid can be added at additional cost.

Prices: Sizes 38 through 50, $149 in wool, $165 in jean cloth.

Confederate Infantry (Foot) Greatcoat

A six-button, single-breasted overcoat with a six-button, closeable cape that reaches to the elbows, the heavy wool Confederate foot greatcoat has a belted back, turned-up cuffs, and an optional stand-up or stand-and-fall collar. The coat is half-lined in wool, its sleeves in cotton. Regulations of 1861 specified a stand-up collar and said "for the present a talma [cape], with sleeves of waterproof material; black."

Considered a burden to carry, greatcoats were usually abandoned early in the war as their owners became acclimated to Northern Virginia winters.

Price: Sizes 36 through 50, $165 in wool, $215 in jean cloth.

Mounted Greatcoat

The mounted overcoat is double-breasted with five buttons on each row. The cape is wrist-length and has a nine-button front. Contrary to 1861 Regulations which call for a stand-up collar, the Grand Illusions collar is stand-and-fall. The back is belted and split to the waist. The coat is half-lined in wool with cotton linings in the sleeves, which end in turn-down cuffs.

Price: Sizes 38 through 52, $198 in wool $245 in jean cloth.

C.S. Military Trousers

These trousers are full-cut in the nineteenth-century manner, with two side-seam pockets, a button fly, six suspender buttons, and an adjustable tie-back.

Price: Sizes 30 through 44, 34-inch length trousers, $68 in wool, $82 in jean cloth.

C.S. Mounted Trousers

Reinforced, per Regulations.

Price: Sizes 30 to 44, $81 in wool, $89 in jean cloth.

C.S. Officer's and N.C.O. Trousers

Also the same as enlisted men's trousers. All sergeants and regimental officers wore these with a 1$1/4$ inch stripe in service colors; medical officers with a black stripe edged in gold braid; and the engineer, commissary quartermaster and adjutant general's departments with a 1-inch gold stripe.

Price: Sizes 28 through 44, $81 in wool, $89 in jean cloth. All trousers are available with mule-ear pockets for an additional charge of $15.

Catalog available, $4.

Grand Illusions Clothing Company
705 Interchange Boulevard
Newark, DE 19711
Phone: 302-366-0300
Fax: 302-738-1858

FEDERAL HEADGEAR
Kepi, Chasseur, or Fatigue Cap

Kepis are the French-inspired caps often worn by officers and men on both sides. While today some reenactors wear their kepis fashionably reversed, the 1860s style was to wear them "pressed-down," with their crossed-sabers badges transferred from front to top, or (as was done later in the war) discarded entirely.

Grand Illusions' Federal enlisted man's version is a copy of "a well-worn artillery officer's kepi," the individual history of which is unknown. The woolen hat is lined in cotton and reinforced with fabric stiffeners. It has a leather brim, sweatband, and a buckled chin strap with brass buttons.

Price: Sizes 6³/4 to 7⁷/8 , $41.

Braided U.S. Officer's Kepi

Taken from a kepi belonging to a captain in the 1st New York Regiment, this chasseur-style cap has three rows of braids on its top and sides. It has a leather chin strap, sweatband, and brim, brass buckle, and eagle buttons.

Price: Sizes 6³/4 to 7³/4 , $41, plus $13.50 to $33.50 for braiding.

Forage or Bummer Caps

In 1858, a board of officers designed the forage cap for general use by the army. The design was adopted in part because it allowed for machine manufacture, reducing cost. During the war, all enlisted men were issued a regulation forage cap of dark blue wool stiffened with buckram and having a pasteboard crown reinforcement, a polished cotton lining, a crescent-shaped leather visor, and two General Service brass buttons. Although they were far less popular with western troops, the only acceptable substitutes for regulation forage caps were those brought into service by private means. Sometimes scorned as "shapeless feedbags," these forage caps stood high on the head and were distinctly unattractive. Nonetheless, this ungainly headgear provided a roomy enough crown for the storage of a wet sponge; the lesser part of a peck of apples; or a small, purloined hen.

Grand Illusions' caps, characterized as "rakish," are fully lined with cotton with fabric stiffeners. Each sports a brim, chin strap and sweatband of leather, and both brass buttons and a buckle.

Price: Sizes 6³/4 to 7³/4 , $39.

Hardee Hats

According to *The Civil War Collector's Encyclopedia,* the Hardee was the most commonly worn hat of the war. The black felt hat had a yellow hatcord and black plume, the latter reserved for parade. On the front was a brass crossed-sabers badge, while the turned-up brim was secured by a brass badge consisting of the U.S. eagle-and-shield.

Despite all this folderol, the Hardees, introduced while Jefferson Davis served as the U.S. Secretary of War under Franklin Pierce, were also referred to as "Jeff Davises." These hats were punched, pulled, and weathered into every configuration imaginable. Soldiers fighting beneath their high felt crowns were soon hot enough to conveniently lose the headgear whenever the opportunity arose. This was not possible for "those black-hatted fellows" of the Iron Brigade, whose commander had his men always wear their Hardees as a distinguishing mark. A variation was the lower-crowned "Burnside" pattern. Per regulation, Grand Illusions' Hardee hats are dressed with cord and insignia.

Prices: Enlisted men's hats, $55. Officers hats, $75.

Catalog available, $4.

Grand Illusions Clothing Company
705 Interchange Boulevard
Newark, DE 19711
Phone: 302-366-0300
Fax: 302-738-1858

Model 1864 Regulation Shako

As used by militias and U.S. Marines. The shako has a black felt body with a recessed enameled crown, bill, and lower band. It was often abandoned in favor of fatigue caps.

Price: $148, brass trim not included

Catalog of "'Hard-To-Find' 19th Century Military Goods & Reproduction Living History Accessories," $6 within the U.S., $10 abroad.

Dixie Leather Works
306 N. 7th Street
Paducah, KY 42001
Phone: 502-442-1058
Fax: 502-442-1049
Order Line: 800-888-5183

Officer's Slouch Hat

The slouch hat emulates the low-crown style of the working man's hat of the eighteenth and nineteenth centuries. When Hungarian patriot Louis Kossuth visited America in 1853 he popularized a softer version of this hat referred to as the "Hungarian," with its brim curled up into a pencil roll and a ribbon band with its short ends hanging off the back. As styles evolved, the low-crown slouch was paired with a medium brim, a grosgrain hatband and a grosgrain-trimmed brim.

This Federal officer's slouch hat was copied directly from a Civil War original.

Catalog of cavalry horse and military equipments, $3.

F. Burgess & Company
200 Pine Place
Red Bank, NJ 07701
Phone: 908-576-1624

CONFEDERATE HEADGEAR

Saying that you'll find none in any of their hats, the Clearwater Hat Company eschews wool. Rather, it claims status as the only hatter in the United States dealing exclusively in period *fur-felt* hats. The company reports that it makes its replica nineteenth-century hats by using original equipment and manufacturing techniques of the era. In their process "the finest pelts … are blended to make a superior fur" and the "softest, strongest, and silkiest underfur is used to form the body." These methods produce a virtually waterproof hat more durable than any made from wool.

In the eighteenth century, it was found that a solution of water and nitric acid could transform inexpensive rabbit pelts into a fair substitute for those of the beleaguered beaver. In the 1790s, hatters refined this formula with the introduction of mercury. During the nineteenth century, mercury worked its alchemy as much inside the hatters' heads as it did outside their hats. Twitching, shuffling, and slurring their speech, they emerged from their mercury-steamed shops into a Wonderland where the lexicon would forever fix them as professionally mad—mad as hatters, all.

Kepi or Chasseur Cap

Although many Southern troops wore kepis to war, these were gradually replaced with slouch hats, which were the fashion—possibly because they afforded greater protection from the elements (see Slouch Hat p. 148). Grand Illusions' replica is fully lined with cotton; has a leather brim, hatband, and chin strap; and a brass buckle and buttons.

Price: Sizes 6³/₄ to 7³/₄, $41.

Forage Cap

Based on an original Confederate forage cap in a private collection, Grand Illusions' replica has a higher crown than the Union version, is fully lined, and has a leather sweatband, chin strap, and brim. This cap can be made with branch-of-service piping.

Price: Sizes 6³/₄ to 7³/₄, $36. $5 additional for piping.

Gold-Braided Officer's Kepi

Trimmed with ¹/₈-inch gold metallic braid in the crown and sides.

Price: Sizes 6³/₄ to 7³/₄, $41, plus $13.50 to $35.50 for braiding.

Catalog of "Historic and Military Reproductions" available, $4.

Grand Illusions Clothing Company
705 Interchange Boulevard
Newark, DE 19711
Phone: 302-366-0300
Fax: 302-738-1858

Mosby Hat

After that worn by J.E.B. Stuart, the curling ostrich plume that Col. John Singleton Mosby used to decorate this hat is remembered as the Confederacy's second most famous.

When he enlisted as a private in the Confederate army, Mosby was a lawyer who came to his profession after having been jailed for shooting a fellow student in a provoked incident at the University of Virginia. By 1862, the 29-year-old cavalryman was a commissioned lieutenant and the scout for Jeb Stuart on his famous June "ride around McClellan" (see Confederate Double-Breasted Shell Jacket p. 141). In January of '63, Mosby was given permission to organize his Partisan Rangers and engage in guerrilla warfare around Northern Virginia's Loudoun Valley. It was there that the rebel officer captured Gen. Edwin H. Stoughton by awakening the Union brigadier in his cot with a slap on the rump and the command "General—get up—dress quick—you are a prisoner."

Described by biographer V.C. Jones as a slight man with medium blond hair, Mosby wore a gray cape lined in scarlet thrown back over his shoulder. His pictures show the aspect of an agile and fearless soldier who was never cruel despite a ruthless determination.

Col. John S. Mosby

During the Wilderness campaign, much Union strength was dedicated to tracking Mosby down, and Jones advances the theory that Mosby's Rangers prolonged the life of the Confederacy by diverting Grant's forces. The futility of these actions was demonstrated during the last winter of the war, when the region known as "Mosby's Confederacy" arose in western Virginia in defiance of Federal countermeasures. Rather than surrender, Colonel Mosby disbanded his Rangers on April 20, 1865 and returned to the practice of law. Mosby died during World War I, having served as U.S. consul in Hong Kong.

Clearwater Hat's Mosby is a flat-crowned ("pork-pie") derby replicating that made famous by the Confederate colonel and his Rangers. It features a leather sweatband and a grosgrain beribboned brim.

Price: $65.

Clearwater Hat Company
Box 202
Newnata, AR 72680
Phone: 501-746-4324

Officers' Unusual Headgear

Stuart and Mosby weren't the only Confederate generals to fight in feathered hats. Jubal Early's headgear was also be-plumed, although with a distinctly non-ostrich-like black feather, while other Southern officers kept out of the sun and rain in variously idiosyncratic ways: Brig. Gen. Albert Pike's headpiece was believed by some to have come from the American Revolution; Texas Gen. Ben McCulloch wore a white felt affair that inspired a reference to him as "a very big and very bald eagle"; while the authentically bald Gen. Joseph E. Johnston, owner of several hats, wore one or another even while at the dinner table.

Union officers who required special toppers to match their individual preferences and exalted status included Brig. Irvin McDowell, who warded off the sun with a hat of bamboo and canvas; Cavalryman Alfred Pleasonton, whose straw hat did the same while imparting "a most jaunty air"; and the millionaire and former French Legionnaire Brig. Gen. Philip Kearny, who, in addition to his gold-braided kepi, sported the uniform of a dandified French nobleman riding out to dazzle his Prussian foe.

Slouch Hat

From Clearwater Hat's Bob Burton:

"The frequent use of slouch hats, especially by Southern soldiers was noted by Bob McDonald, in an article published in the Christmas, 1991 issue of *North/South Trader's Civil War*. In this he states: 'We now have a limited amount of data of headdress of the Army of Northern Virginia in the field in 1862, 1863, and 1864. In each sample, the slouch hat is the most common headgear … In addition to this … in-the-field photographs of Confederate troops … indicate the strong numerical superiority of slouch hats over caps.'"

Price: $65.

Gettysburg Hat

This hat, with its telescoping crown, is found in many Civil War-era photographs. It has a smaller, curled brim and period leather sweatband. Lining, tippet, and a grosgrain brim are included.

Price: $75.

The Clearwater Hat Company's period headgear also includes derby, plantation, bell-crowned, top, carriage, hardee, plug, beehive, ladies' riding and panama hats. They come in five colors—black, "coffee," "pecan," tan, and steel gray in sizes ranging from 6$1/2$ to 8 inches.

Mailer and price list available.

Clearwater Hat Company
Box 202
Newnata, AR 72680
Phone: 501-746-4324

BOOTS

1859 Jefferson Boot

The unprecedented demand for shoes caused by the Civil War industrialized their manufacture. Generally, the "bootees" issued to troops were better than their civilian counterparts, and made for shoes that had "plenty of room to spare in all directions," according to one soldier, "except in one or two places where they pinched."

Considering how poorly the shoes fared in water, their nicknames mysteriously listed towards the nautical, with "gunboats," "ferry-boats," and "pontoons" representing a fair selection. Certainly these mudscows were big, but the virtues imposed by their size were of the earthbound sort, with another soldier swearing that one of his was not only large enough to sleep in, but that after placing a piece of brown paper on it he "improvised a satisfactory writing desk."

The brogans depicted came as rights and lefts, unlike the straight-last types that preceded them. Other changes included a shortening of the upper so that it came to just above the ankle, and a reduction of the lace holes from five or six to four. Available in black and russet.

Price: $139, the pair. (If bought within the Confederacy in 1864, these shoes would've cost nearly the same.)

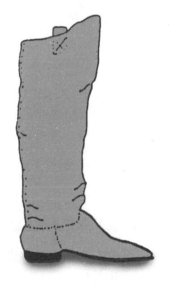

1861 Cavalry Boot

This boot, used by both Union and Confederate cavalry units, is characterized by square toes, a back seam, and a scalloped knee guard. Made of horse- or mule hide, with a lining of leather. The heel is stacked leather. Available in black or russet.

Price: $255, the pair.

1862 Cavalry Knee Boot

Available in either officer or enlisted man's models.

Price: $215, the pair.

1860 Jeb Stuart Style Hip Boot

Following the type "popularized by many of the boy generals of the Civil War," these boots should be measured to rise to two or three inches below the crotch.

Price: $385, the pair.

Brochure of replica military boots available, $2.

Except in instances where the original was made of a different, more readily available leather, all of Cavalry Regimental Supply's boots are authentically fashioned from horse or mule hide.

Cavalry Regimental Supply
Box 64394
Lubbock, TX 79464
Fax: 806-798-8867

Similar goods obtainable from:

Montana Boot Company
P.O. Box 77
Livingston, MT 59047
Phone: 406-222-7723

Woolen Socks & Gloves

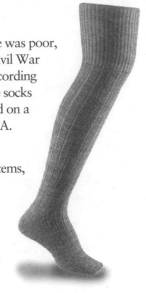

All I have to say is what the girl said when she stuck her foot into the stocking. It strikes me there's something in it.

—Abraham Lincoln on September 13, 1861, after viewing a model of the first ironclad.

According to a story making the rounds in camp, late in '62 a soldier in the 92nd Illinois searched in vain for his socks. Exasperated, he resolved to go ahead and bathe his feet anyway. After washing away "one thickness of dirt" he found the socks, covering over the additional layers of real estate that had attached themselves to his feet.

As material used in government-issue was poor, the best socks and gloves worn by Civil War soldiers were those knit at home. According to Panther Primitives, machine-made socks like the ones depicted here were listed on a period poster for the company of W.A. Jones, New York.

Catalog of Early American frontier items, $2.

Panther Primitives
P.O. Box 32
Normantown, WV 25267
Phone: 304-462-7718
Order Line: 800-467-2684

Military Fabrics

County Cloth has a complete line of museum-grade, replica military fabrics available for immediate shipment. These include both domet and blouse flannels, kerseys (lightweight woolens that have a cotton warp), satinettes (cotton and wool cloths made to resemble satin), tickings, checks, and broadcloths. Also obtainable from the Ohio firm are what it considers to be "the most extensive line of jeans, based on some of the earliest research on the subject." In keeping with County Cloth's dedication to authenticity, all these precisely duplicate the color, thread count, and finish of the original fabrics upon which they are based.

Price list for replica military blankets, fabrics and garment kits available with swatch card, $5.

County Cloth
13797-C Georgetown Street, N.E.
Paris, OH 44669
Phone: 330-862-3307
Fax: 330-862-3304

WAGONS

You might buy a Lincoln, but when Lincoln needed vehicles, he bought Studebakers. At least it was the Studebaker factory at South Bend, Indiana, that supplied the Federal Army with most of its thousands of ambulances, and supply and battery wagons. In a geographical distribution that overwhelmingly favored the North, other major carriage manufacturers were located in Massachusetts, Connecticut, New York, and New Jersey.

The typical war wagon was built of seasoned hickory and ash, its wheels sturdy enough to endure the worst "Confederate" weather and most difficult terrain. Canvas tops were regulation, and seldom removed.

Early in the war the Union Quartermaster Corps established a number of huge "wagon parks"—staging areas like the one in Brady Station Virginia, where wagons were repaired, mules shod, and equipment generally readied for battle. From these, supply wagons coordinated with the major railroad centers to move men and materiel forward as the lines of battle shifted. As Civil War soldiers were literally "on the march," the Studies and other wagons were rarely used as personnel carriers.

Full-scale replicas of Civil War wagons are being custom built today by William Lee Green. Mr. Green's enterprise is associated with a private museum that features a 1929 tourist home, gas station, and a White Castle, but he has sold his nineteenth-century-style wagons to other historical sites, including those at the Oregon Trail Interpretive Center and Fort Scott, Kansas.

For further information contact:

Green's Carriage Restoration & Heritage Museum
10530 Thrailkill Road
Orient, OH 43146
Phone: 614-877-4254
Fax: 614-983-2566

Horses & Mules

Half a mile, half a mile,
Half a mile onward
Right through the Georgia troops
Broke the two hundred.
"Forward the Mule Brigade!
Charge for the Rebs!" they neighed.
Straight for the Georgia troops,
Broke the two hundred.

…

Mules to the right of them,
Mules to the left of them,
Mules behind them
Pawed, neighed and thundered.
Breaking their own confines,
Breaking through Longstreet's lines
Into the Georgia troops,
Stormed the two hundred.

The "Charge of the Mule Brigade," a soldier's parody of Alfred Lord Tennyson's "Charge of the Light Brigade," celebrates the engagement—probably apocryphal—known as the Wauhatchie Night Attack. This 10 p.m. raid, which was itself a part of the 1863 Chattanooga campaign, involved the repulse of men under the command of Confederate Gen.

Evander Law, by 200 U.S. army mules. As described by U.S. Grant, the terrified mules (who had been abandoned by their skinners) blindly charged into Law's advancing lines. Spooked by the maneuver, Law's men then "stampeded in turn," leaving the field to the pack animals. In recognition of their uncommon valor, someone recommended that the mules be breveted as horses.

Unfortunately, the opportunities for such glorious displays of hybrid heroism as witnessed at Wauhatchie have been few. Nonetheless, as an Illinois soldier's 1864 description of another battle zone reveals, the Civil War mule's opportunities to make the ultimate sacrifice were, conversely, great: "Let people talk about thare balm of a thousand flower," he wrote, "but we can beat that heare. We have the balm of a thousand mules. The roads are strewn with dead mules. It beats any thing I ever hurd tell of."

Don Smith, with the 51st Alabama Partisan Rangers, offers horses and mules familiar only with the horrors of reenactment.

Dixie Horse & Mule Company
Wicksburg, AL 36352
Phone: 334-692-5665

Civil War-Pattern Headstall

Shown with accompanying reins and link strap. Features black frame buckles.

Catalog of cavalry horse and military equipments, $3.

F. Burgess & Company
200 Pine Place
Red Bank, NJ 07701
Phone: 908-576-1624

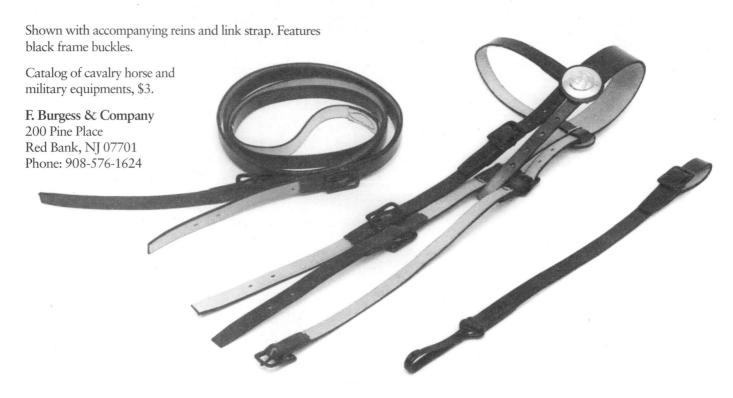

Wool Valise

As used by dragoon officers, this cylindrical valise is designed to fit close behind the saddle. It is available in blue or gray wool, and is canvas-lined with black or yellow trim. Hardware is brass horseshoe buckles with beveled edges.

Price: $85; leather-trimmed officer's model, $95.

1812-1865 Double Holsters

Copied from a pattern in the Smithsonian collection, these holsters fit over the pommel of a saddle. They can be made for single-shot flint pistols; cap-and-ball pistols; 1849 Walker revolvers; 1st, 2nd, 3rd, model Colt Dragoons and the 1860 Army. The thick leather holsters have straps, brass bottom-caps, and a cartridge pouch located under each flap. Enlisted men's versions have leather plugs in place of the brass bottom-caps.

Price: Officer's double holster, $150; with black bear fur on flaps, $170. Price for enlisted men's double holster, $130.

Catalog of replica Civil War leather goods available, $3.

Border States Leatherworks
1158 Apple Blossom Lane
Springdale, AR 72762
Phone: 501-361-2642
Fax: 501-361-2851 (orders only)

Patten's Cavalry Drill & Sabre Exercise

by George Washington Patten

The cumbersome three-volume 1841 *Cavalry Tactics* manual (a.k.a. "Poinsett's Tactics") was the standard maneuver reference for the mounted service until 1874. *Patten's Cavalry Drill & Sabre Exercise* (1861) is a digest version of this venerable set designed for use by volunteer cavalrymen. A vest pocket edition as was the original, it has been bound in the same light-blue paper stock. This is a reprint of the Union edition, which differed from its Southern counterpart only in that it was published in New York rather than Richmond.

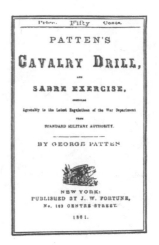

Federal-Issue M-1859 Nose Bag

"An exacting replica based on a thorough survey of many extant martially-marked originals." As original billet specifications may prove too short for horses with larger heads, Heartland House preserves the integrity of its replica by requiring the owners of such horses to request a billet extension, as would have been done during the war. Available in cotton or linen.

U. S. Army Bucket

As patented in 1861 by one R.B. Fitts, this contraption was designed to double as a portable water bucket and nose bag. Rugged construction (heavy cotton duck with a rope reinforced mouth) and collapsibility are its salient features. Distinguished among buckets as that which enjoyed the endorsement of Quartermaster Gen. M.C. Meigs, its replica includes a facsimile reprint of the original promotional flyer (the source of the accompanying illustration).

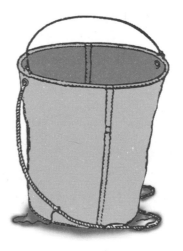

Heartland House
Old Blue Ridge Turnpike
Rochelle, VA 22738
Phone & Fax: 540-672-9267

C.S. Government Grain Sack

Features Confederate States stencil and assistant quartermaster's inspection stamp. Copied from an original in the collection of the Gettysburg National Park Service.

Catalog of "Saddlery, Horse Equipments, and Equestriana of Every Description" available.

Heartland House
Old Blue Ridge Turnpike
Rochelle, VA 22738
Phone & Fax: 540-672-9267

U.S. Cavalry Saddle Blanket

Orders from the U.S. Ordnance Department dated July 19, 1858 require and describe a complete set of horse equipments. Saddle blankets, according to regulations, were "to be of pure wool, close woven, of stout yarns of an indigo blue color, with an orange border 3 inches wide, 3 inches from the edge." Conforming in all respects save for its eight extra inches of length and lack of a six-inch "U.S." legend, the saddle blanket produced by Hamilton Dry Goods of Cookeville, Tennessee measures 83 by 67 inches. This blanket was used by the cavalry early into the twentieth century, when it was replaced by an olive drab version.

Price: $79. Dealer discounts available.

"Tailor's Guide," a brochure depicting a line of "historically correct clothing patterns—colonial, fur trade, Civil War, western frontier," obtainable upon request.

Hamilton Dry Goods
2510 Randolph Road
Cookeville, TN 38506
Phone: 615-528-6061

SADDLES

McClellan Saddles

But McClellan is nevertheless the 'man on horseback' just now, and the Americans must ride in his saddle, or in anything he likes.

—William Howard Russell, *My Diary North and South*, 1863.

Prior to '63, George Brinton McClellan did ride tall in the saddle, which, according to his preference, followed a Hungarian design. Hailed as the Union's "Young Napoleon" at the start of the war, McClellan proved himself a genius at military organization, administration, and in the training of men who cheered his every appearance. Easily as vainglorious as his nick-namesake, McClellan couldn't muster the mettle for a decent Waterloo. In vain, Lincoln said he would gladly hold McClellan's horse "if he will only bring us success."

When McClellan had been commander of the Department of the Ohio, a triumph at Rich Mountain, Virginia brought him to prominence just before the Federal disaster at First Bull Run. Years before, as the boyish vice-president of the Illinois Central, Little Mac had made Lincoln's acquaintance while the future president was one of the railroad's lawyers. While this association may have figured into McClellan's ill-disguised contempt for Lincoln, it may have also had some bearing on his getting the command of the armies surrounding Washington—and, soon thereafter, of all the armies of the North. Having replaced the venerable Winfield ("One Year Older than the Constitution") Scott in this exalted position, McClellan's first job was the Peninsular campaign, which sought to capture Richmond via a long march up from the sea.

On his campaigns, McClellan had a horse named Burns, the gift and namesake of an army friend. Each evening at dinnertime, Burns (the horse) would always bolt for his oats heedless of any desire on his master's part to remain seated where he was. It is therefore a wonder that no one ever thought to place Burns' dinner ever closer to Richmond during the Peninsular campaign. Little Mac's failure on the Peninsula resulted in the loss of his command (and the addition of another embarrassing sobriquet—"the Virginia Creeper"—to his growing list of unfortunate nicknames), but the Second Confederate victory at Bull Run proved as lucky for him as the first, and his command was restored after Gen. "Saddle-Bag" John Pope's defeat there (see "Saddlebags," below). Reinstalled as commander of the Army of the Potomac, McClellan again exasperated the administration with his avoidance of the enemy. After failing to pursue Lee at Antietam, McClellan finally lost Lincoln's forbearance, and with it his command.

For the 1864 presidential campaign in which McClellan ran against Lincoln, the president's well-remembered slogan was "Don't Change Horses in Midstream." Fortunately for the Union cause, the country didn't. And McClellan's saddle, having become so prettily burnished during his military days, stayed entirely dry.

F. Burgess & Company's McClellan saddles are of the highest repute, having been made on wooden trees to replicate the originals. In the same way, they are covered with the best rawhide and rigged with the best vegetable-tanned leather. Stirrups, coat straps, skirts, and fenders are included. The company offers an early-war, 1859-Pattern McClellan featuring hooded oak stirrups; and a late-war 1864 Pattern with japanned hardware, "spaded" D-rings, unhooded stirrups, and an inspector's stamp on the cantle.

Catalog of cavalry horse and military equipments, $3.

F. Burgess & Company
200 Pine Place
Red Bank, NJ 07701
Phone: 908-576-1624

1847 Grimsley Saddle

Although designed as an enlisted man's dragoon saddle, pictorial evidence shows the 1847 Grimsley to have been used by many officers on both sides during the Civil War. Border States Leatherworks' copy is authentically double-skirted, with deer-hair padding and the correct polished brass stirrups suspended from hand-forged hangers. The saddle's tree is properly made of wood, and although made to fit modern horses, measures 14 inches as per the originals. All Grimsley saddles come complete with correct girth, coat straps, valise straps, and authentic brass beveled-edge horseshoe buckles.

Price: $1,070.

Catalog of Civil War leather goods available, $3.

Border States Leatherworks
1158 Apple Blossom Lane
Springdale, AR 72762
Phone: 501-361-2642
Fax: 501-361-2851 (orders only)

Texas Saddle

Championed for official military use by Confederate General Joseph E. Johnston, the Texas saddle was in fact procured from the commercial market by Federal agents and issued to troops as the "Ranger" saddle. Southern authorities also sanctioned the issue of the Texas saddle as an interim measure while the C.S.-manufactured McClellan was still being developed early in '64. The Heartland House's citizen version incorporates features typical of examples bearing mid-nineteenth-century provenance: it is built on a rawhide tree and trimmed in the Mexican style. It is three-quarter seated and detailed with ornamental brass-headed saddle nails. It comes complete with a lampwick girth, stirrup leathers, and wooden stirrups fitted with leather hoods and covered treads. Available with "western" saddle seats.

Catalog of "Saddlery, Horse Equipments, and Equestriana of Every Description" available.

Heartland House
Old Blue Ridge Turnpike
Rochelle, VA 22738
Phone & Fax: 540-672-9267

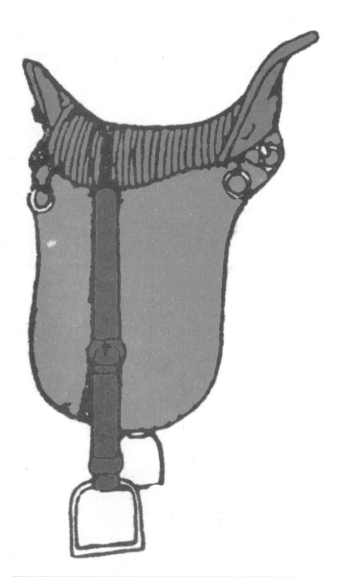

SPURS

Union & Confederate Spurs

These spurs are of solid brass and fitted with white metal rowels. The Southern spurs are of the Richmond Tredegar pattern, commonly found at the sites of the Confederate encampments surrounding the capital.

Price: Union-issue spurs, $26.60, Confederate-issue spurs, $30.

Catalog of Civil War leather goods available.

The Cavalry Shop
9700 Royerton Drive
Richmond, VA 23228
Phone: 804-266-0898

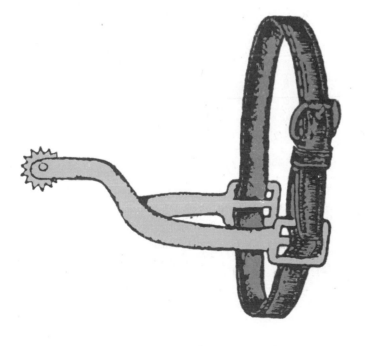

Memphis Novelty Works Spurs

This model was styled on the Model 1859 Federal-issue spurs, themselves a variant of the standard U.S. pattern. Confederate spurs of this type are generally attributed to the Memphis Novelty Works of Memphis, Tennessee and Columbus, Georgia. Straight-necked Richmond-Depot pattern spurs also available.

Catalog of "Saddlery, Horse Equipments, and Equestriana of Every Description" available.

Heartland House
Old Blue Ridge Turnpike
Rochelle, VA 22738
Phone & Fax: 540-672-9267

SADDLEBAGS

1859 Saddlebags

Pope was saddled with the title of 'Saddle-bag John' in memory of his famous order about head-quarters being on horseback.

— *Centennial Magazine*, October, 1884.

The wartime quip was that Pope's headquarters were where his hindquarters should have been. Even so, it was not until late in the Second Battle of Bull Run that Pope lost control of the situation, and then only after being confronted by the devastating combination of Stonewall Jackson's troops moving in concert with Lee's "strategic envelopment."

F. Burgess' saddlebags include an 1859 pattern of the type that saw military service through the 1880s, and an 1859 officer's bag, featuring the yellow piping and brass buckles with which Pope may have been familiar.

Catalog of cavalry horse and military equipments, $3.

F. Burgess & Company
200 Pine Place
Red Bank, NJ 07701
Phone: 908-576-1624

Confederate Large Saddlebags

These saddlebags were fashioned from an original in the collection belonging to Dixie Leather Works. It consists of two large bags, the oversized flaps of which are secured with three straps apiece. Thought to have seen use in the Confederate cavalry and later in the Indian Wars, the bags' replicas are made from top-grain cowhide.

Price: $145.

Available in black and brown leather.

Catalog of "Hard-To-Find' 19th Century Military Goods & Reproduction Living History Accessories," $6 within the U.S., $10 abroad.

Dixie Leather Works
306 N. 7th Street
Paducah, KY 42001
Phone: 502-442-1058
Fax: 502-442-1049
Order Line: 800-888-5183

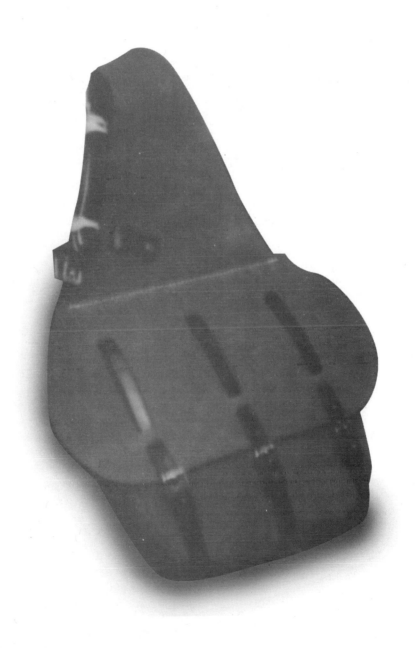

In its use of French words, the battlefield isn't a very long way from the bistro. During the Civil War era in particular, French terms claimed a panache more likely derived from Napoleon's military campaigns than from nuanced descriptions of the *délassements culinaires* served at the party for Lamartine's *Méditations poétiques*. The word accoutrement (here, the Civil War spelling is used) is a Gallicism that has been universally adopted to refer to military items (other than weapons and uniforms) that are carried by soldiers. While the term usually indicates belts and the boxes, slings, and scabbards they carry—it sometimes also refers to knapsacks, haversacks, and canteens.

HAVERSACKS & KNAPSACKS

When in the field, each soldier would carry his rations in a haversack made of either canvas or leather. In theory these were waterproof affairs, but a downpour would usually render them as ineffective as any cloth bag. The effect that this would have both on the haversack's contents and the bag itself (most were issued white) were barely tolerable, even by a foot soldier's standards. As one wrote: "By the time one of these haversacks had been in use for a few weeks as a receptacle for chunks of fat bacon and fresh meat, damp sugar tied up in a rag—perhaps a piece of an old shirt—potatoes and other vegetables that might be picked up along the route, it took on the color of a printing-office towel."

Single Bag Confederate Knapsack

Many Confederate soldiers used blanket rolls and home-made cloth satchels in lieu of knapsacks. This knapsack is described by Dixie Leather as per C.S. Issue. It features a black top-grain cowhide body, and heavy leather reinforcements and straps.

Outside dimensions: 14 inches high by 17 inches wide by 4 1/2 inches deep.

Price: $132.

Adjutant's Hardpack Knapsack also obtainable.

Militia Hardpack Knapsack

Among his accoutrements, the Civil War soldier was issued a knapsack to carry such belongings as a double wool blanket, a half-shelter tent and a rubber blanket. Even after they were stripped to these bare necessities, knapsacks were so burdensome that, as one observer commented, " the headiest pack-horses in the world would break down under the heavy, sagging, illy-adjusted loads borne by our soldiers."

Used from the Mexican War through the War for Southern Independence, when it was worn by soldiers on both sides, this is considered by its maker to be the classic Civil War knapsack. Per the original, it has a waterproof canvas body that is mounted on a wooden frame, both of which are covered by a leather flap. The knapsack is handcrafted using the "finest-quality leather available."

Dimensions: 15 inches square by 4 inches deep.

Price: $140. Regimental number, company letter, and soldier's number provided by customer will be applied by hand in white oil paint with the originals in the correct lettering for an additional $8. The bedroll and leather blanket shown in accompanying photograph are not included or available.

Catalog of "'Hard-To-Find' 19th Century Military Goods & Reproduction Living History Accessories," $6 within the U.S., $10 abroad.

Dixie Leather Works
306 N. 7th Street
Paducah, KY 42001
Phone: 502-442-1058
Fax: 502-442-1049
Order Line: 800-888-5183

Officer's Haversack

As depicted in Lord's *Encyclopedia*, this is a large single-pocket haversack 12½ inches wide and 11½ inches deep. It is made of top-grain cowhide and features a pocket on the front flap.

Price: $108.

Carry-All haversack also available.

Catalog of "'Hard-To-Find' 19th Century Military Goods & Reproduction Living History Accessories," $6 within the U.S., $10 abroad.

Dixie Leather Works
306 N. 7th Street
Paducah, KY 42001
Phone: 502-442-1058
Fax: 502-442-1049
Order Line: 800-888-5183

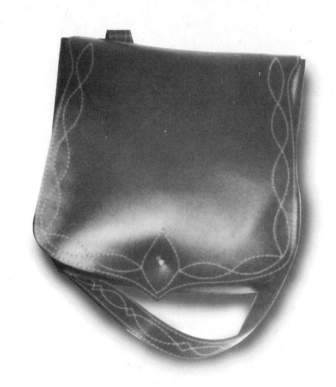

U.S. Tarred Haversack

The Cavalry Shop's U.S. tarred haversack is made from heavy, canvas-like linen. It is has a removable linen liner, wooden buttons, and a covering flap.

Price: $26.50.

Plain tarred, and gunner's haversack also available.

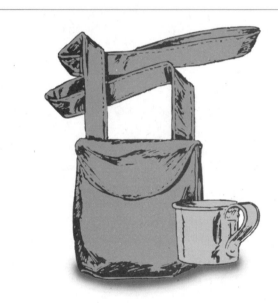

Pistol Holsters

According to Alfred Lord's *Encyclopedia*, Civil War belt holsters varied "according to the size and model of the pistol or revolver it held." While specifying holsters for the Colt Walker and LeMat revolvers, Richmond's Cavalry Shop will supply holsters to fit any Civil War weapon.

Price: Walker and LeMat holsters, $24.50 each.

Catalog of "Quality Leather Goods for Collectors and Skirmishers" available.

The Cavalry Shop
9700 Royerton Drive
Richmond, VA 23228
Phone: 804-266-0898

North Carolina Depot Canteen

This canteen authentically reproduces the F.J. Gardner design specifically called for by many Civil War contracts. Replicated from a North Carolina original, it is handmade of white cedar that has been shellacked and lined with beeswax. The canteen's sides are concave and it has a wooden spout and stopper that is attached to one of its three metal sling hoops with a rawhide strip.

Measurements: Diameter, 7$\frac{1}{4}$ inches; thickness, 1$\frac{1}{2}$ inches.

Price: $55.

Fort Branch Supply's Ken Bucher also has Civil War-era wooden trunks available in various sizes.

Fort Branch Supply
Post Office Box 222
Hamilton, NC 27840
Phone: 919-798-2671

Tin Canteen

This canteen, which takes its dimensions from one excavated at Harper's Ferry, measures approximately 7 inches in diameter. It has a chain-held stopper and a mattress ticking sling retained by brass wire holders. The canteen is made with lead-free solder and is lined with beeswax.

Price: $27.50.

Catalog specializing in period tinware available.

The Village Tinsmithing Works
P.O. Box 189
Randolph, OH 44265
Phone: 330 325 9101

Similar items obtainable from:

P.M. Cunningham, Tinner
402 East Main Street
Madison, IN 47250
Phone: 812-273-4193

CARTRIDGE BOXES

Blakeslee Cartridge Box

This box, used by some cavalry, was patented on December 20, 1864 by Erastus Blakeslee of Plymouth, Connecticut. The Border States replica has a leather box containing an inner block of wood wrapped in tin. It has six removable tubes, each accepting original-size ammunition. An implement pouch and shoulder strap are included.

Price: $215.

Catalog of 19th-Century Military Leather Goods, $3.

Border States Leatherworks
1158 Apple Blossom Lane
Springdale, AR 72762
Phone: 501-361-2642
Fax: 501-361-2851 (orders only)

U.S. & C.S. Army Cartridge Boxes

Asserting that they are made in accordance with U.S. ordnance regulations, the Cavalry Shop also claims that many of its cartridge boxes incorporate original Civil War finials. The .58 to .69 caliber boxes are fashioned from high-grade leather in either natural, black, or "Confederate" russet. All have either brass or copper metal parts, and contain pockets for patches.

Price: $36.50.

Enfield Cartridge Box

While most Confederate cartridge boxes had the same general proportions as their U.S. counterparts, the leather was actually of a different quality. Many Southern cartridge boxes used were also of English manufacture, having come over as part of the equipments accompanying the Enfield muskets and rifles. The Cavalry Shop's Enfield cartridge boxes follow the size and pattern of the originals, including a back strap. Available in russet or black.

Price: $36.

U.S. Officer's Belt

Of the type popular with Northern officers and cavalry, for use with two-piece buckle. Special-order belts with square or oval sword rings are available.

Price: $16.50.

Cavalry Belt & Accoutrements

Made of American strap leather with brass and copper pieces, this cavalry (and artillery) belt is available in black, "Confederate" russet, and natural-tanned leather. Included are Confederate or state buckles, a cartridge box, holster, and straps.

Price: Full rig with buckle, $96; for officer's rig, $114.

Binocular Case

"Civil War Style," with shoulder strap. Available embossed "US" or "CS," in black or brown.

Price: $65.

Catalog of "Quality Leather Goods for Collectors and Skirmishers" available.

The Cavalry Shop
9700 Royerton Drive
Richmond, VA 23228
Phone: 804-266-0898

MAPS, FLAGS & ESPIONAGE EQUIPMENT

Roll-Up Map or Document Case

Black leather case measures 14 inches long by 15 inches wide and has an adjustable strap closure and handle. Available in black leather only.

Price: $48.50.

Cylindrical map and dispatch cases also obtainable.

Catalog of "'Hard-To-Find' 19th Century Military Goods & Reproduction Living History Accessories," $6 U.S., $10 abroad.

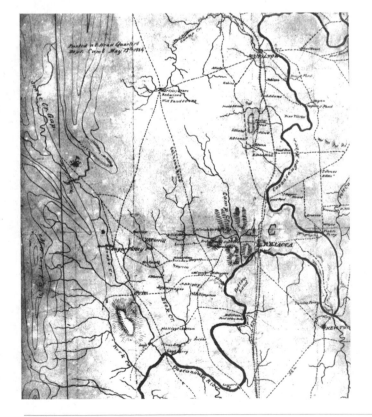

Topographical Maps

Replicas of maps drawn in 1869 to include rivers, railroads, forts, abatis, cities, and towns of what had been the Eastern and Trans-Mississippi theaters. Included are maps of Fredericksburg, Culpepper and Appomattox, Virginia; Vicksburg and Corinth, Mississippi; Chattanooga south to Kennesaw Mountain; and Atlanta east to Savannah, Georgia. Size, 11 by 17 inches.

Price: $2.25 each, five for $10.

Dixie Leather Works
306 N. 7th Street
Paducah, KY 42001
Phone: 502-442-1058
Fax: 502-442-1049
Order Line: 800-888-5183

Federal Flags

With the addition of West Virginia, the U.S. flag gained a star during the Civil War, while at the same time relinquishing none of the eleven that considered themselves part of a new confederacy. This was a provocation on the battlefield, where flags are national symbols in perilous circumstances. For each side, advancing the flag while at the same time defending it from capture took on a meaning that transcended military success.

Frontier Flags of Thermopolis, Wyoming, produces seven varieties of the 34- and 35-star U.S. national flags flown during the Civil War. These range in size from 36 by 39 inches to 6 by 6½ feet, and in prices from $159.95 to $249.95. With the exception of the 60 by 72-inch cotton flag with 35 sewn stars, all are made from silk and show painted stars.

Also available are three of Gen. George Armstrong Custer's personal battle flags for the period 1863-1865. The first (July-October, 1863) of these swallowtail banners with their red-over-blue, saber-crossed bars, replicates one made in the field, which used the discarded clothing of soldiers.

Free catalog of replicated Union, Confederate, regimental, and other historic American flags available.

Frontier Flags
1761 Owl Creek Route
Thermopolis, WY 82443
Phone: 307-867-2551
Order line: 800-921-9218

Confederate Flags

The Hebrew poet whose idea of awe-inspiring was expressed by the phrase 'terrible as an army with banners' [doubtless] had his view from the top of a mountain.

—Confederate Gen. Harvey Hill before the Battle of South Mountain, September, 1862.

According to Larry Miller of Authentic Reproductions, all of his company's flags are custom-made on a per-order basis. Using cotton throughout, the company's sewers are devoted to making the flags as true to their original counterparts as possible.

Prices:

Bonnie Blue	$ 145
First Confederate National	$ 145
Battle Flag	$ 165
Cavalry version, 32" x 32"	$ 112
Artillery version, 38" x 38"	$ 140
Infantry version, 51" x 51"	$ 200
Second Confederate National	$ 170
Third Confederate National	$ 170

Authentic Reproductions
1031 Old Nankin Road, R-3
Ashland, OH 44805
Phone: 419-289-6642 or 419-289-8688
Fax: 419-289-8688

The Confederate Battle Flag

"On they come," wrote a witness to one of the Civil War's most civil—and poignant—moments, *"with the old swinging route-step and swaying battle-flags."*

They came on an April morning, days after Robert E. Lee's surrender to U.S. Grant, marching into Appomattox for a ceremonial laying down of arms. Led by Confederate Gen. John Gordon, the first unit in their line of march was the vaunted Stonewall Brigade, now reduced to some 200 men. For the northern troops lining the road, the gray tableau was relieved by the Confederates' crimson battle flags, "crowded so thick, by thinning out of men," wrote Union Brigadier Joshua Chamberlain, "that the whole column seemed crowned with red."

Gen. Gordon rode high in his saddle, but with his head bowed and his expression grim. As he and his men passed through their former enemy's ranks, a doleful silence permeated the scene. Looking on, Chamberlain was reminded of "the passing of the dead."

Suddenly, the quiet was broken by the shout of a Union command and the clatter of muskets rising to shoulder. Gordon wheeled his mount in alarm. The general and his war horse knew an ambush when they heard one, but it took a moment to savvy that this was no ordinary bushwhacking. Rearing his charger so they formed "one uplifted figure," Gordon acknowledged the Union salute with a sweep of his

sword and barked a command of his own. In a flash of its former glory, the Army of Northern Virginia snapped to shoulder arms, acknowledging the Union tribute in kind.

The exchange was, in Chamberlain's words, "honor answering honor." When it passed, the vanquished Confederates faced the Union general, dressed their lines, fixed their bayonets, stacked their arms, and 'Lastly — and reluctantly, with agony of expression — they fold their flags, battle-worn, and torn, bloodstained, heart-holding colors, and lay them down.'

In what nation other than the United States would the flag that waged war against it flourish? Will the Red Chinese produce souvenirs of the Tianamen Square uprising? Should a Kurdish Stonewall Jackson rise and fall, will Saddam Hussein erect statues in his memory? For all that attests to America's fascination with its own Civil War, nothing is so telling as the modern adoption of the secessionist's red banner. This flag—*the battle flag of the Confederacy*—is today the country's second most popular.

The flag is often mistakenly referred to as the "Stars and Bars"—which is actually the name of the South's first *national* flag. That flag, proposed by the Confederate government's Committee on the Flag and Seal under William Porcher Miles, was an Old-Glory lookalike reflecting "a strange and earnest desire to retain … a suggestion of the old Stars and Stripes."

To do so, it employed three horizontal bands of red and white offset by a blue canton, within which a circle of seven white stars represented the first states to secede from the Union. The Stars and Bars rose over the Confederacy's Montgomery, Alabama capitol in time for Lincoln's March 4, 1861, inaugural—but its baptism under fire had to wait until July 21, when First Bull Run was fought. It was also the day during which the Confederacy's now-familiar battle flag was conceived.

Before First Bull Run's last engagement, Gen. Pierre G.T. Beauregard, Commander of the Confederate Army of the Potomac, watched through field glasses as an unknown body of soldiers advanced upon his left flank. Unable to tell if the flag these men carried through the sultry air was the Federal Stars and Stripes or its Confederate counterpart, Beauregard called for reinforcements from his Departmental Commander, Joseph E. Johnston. As he awaited the arrival of these on his right, Beauregard received information that the large column opposite was likely a Northern force. Were this true, the Yankees would surely arrive before reinforcements could, annihilating Beauregard's troops, and ending all prospects for an historic defeat of Lincoln's army.

Nevertheless, Beauregard held his ground. Suddenly, a breeze arose to reveal that the mysterious flag bearing down on him was not only Confederate, but that it was carried by a large force under the command of Gen. Jubal Early. With the tables now turned in his favor, Beauregard bid his staff to "see that the day is ours" and ordered the advance that eventually routed Federal forces clear to Washington. However, that the day *was* his didn't deter the Louisianan from addressing its harrowing confusion.

Beauregard enlisted the aid of a staff colonel to design a distinctive battle flag such as those used by British regiments for centuries. The colonel was the same William P. Miles whose committee had produced the Confederate national flag months before. Then, Miles' preference was for a banner showing a blue saltier—or St. Andrew's cross—in which two arms of equal length bisected like the letter "X." As it bore insufficient resemblance to the U.S. flag (and was ridiculed by one legislator as looking like "a pair of suspenders") the Confederate congress rejected it. However, with a distinctive flag now needed, Miles presented his sawbuck-shaped cross again.

This was not the first time that someone had pressed the saltire into hard duty. Before his death in A.D. 60, Saint Andrew is said to have asked his persecutors to spare him the blasphemy of recreating Christ's crucifixion by turning his cross on its side. In his torment, Andrew joyously preached the gospel—an act that has made his oblique cross a straightforward Church symbol of martyrdom. In A.D. 750, Andrew became patron saint of Scotland, where his cross has informed the flag ever since. The Scottish saltire was incorporated into

4th Regiment of the Georgia Volunteers with "Stars and Bars" flag.

By the end of 1863, the Confederate battle flag's cross of St. Andrew had been placed into the national flag's canton.

the flag for the United Kingdoms of England and Scotland in 1606. To further recommend it to Southerners, this composite became the canton on the patriot "Grand Union Flag" used by Gen. George Washington in 1776.

Back at his Fairfax headquarters, Beauregard discussed Miles' design with Capt. J.B. Walton and General Johnston. They considered other proposals, but in the end chose the familiar "A.N.V." (for "Army of Northern Virginia" as the southern Army of the Potomac later became known) pattern battle flag that today reminds Italians of Elvis. That fall, three Baltimore belles—Hetty and Jennie Cary, and their "magnetic" cousin Constance, sang the secessionist "Maryland! My Maryland!" for Beauregard, who was magnetized enough to commission the young women in a regiment created for the occasion and named "The Cary Invincibles." That Constance would later marry an aide to President Jefferson Davis may or may not have had something to do with why, weeks later, they were asked to execute silken versions of the first new battle flags by a congressional commission. To save material, the Cary Invincibles set the flag's blue St. Andrew's cross on a *square* field of red. The banner bore twelve white stars—eleven for states then in the Confederacy, and one for Missouri, the status of which was still a matter of some belligerence.

Around November of 1861, when A.N.V. troops mustered in Centreville, Virginia for the presentation of their battle flag, a poem found "in some old Catholic Monastery in Maryland somewhere" appeared in the *Washington Evening Star*. Its antiquity was questionable, but the reference it appeared to make to the battle flag must have aroused interest among the banner's celebrants:

Ere thirteen united
Are thrice what they were
Shall the Eagle be blighted
By the fortunes of war.

When sixty is ended
And one takes its place
Then shall brothers offended
Deal mutual disgrace.

But whenever the Cross
Takes its place mid the Stars
They shall gain by their loss
And thus end all their wars.

Reading like the Confederate Vision of Nostradamus, the poem portended much for the battle flag, which, given its *nom de guerre* "Southern Cross," had seemed to enjoy a mystical significance from its inception.

After the presentation, the Confederate quartermaster ordered 120 battle flags for the Army of Northern Virginia. They were made of dress silk purchased on the open market. As red was in short supply, varying shades of pink silk were substituted. The yellow-bordered flags were made by volunteer sewing circles in Richmond and were distributed to the troops at the end of 1861. The A.N.V. battle flag was adopted with acclaim by virtually all the armies of the Confederacy's Eastern and Trans-Mississippi theaters. By the end of 1863, it had replaced the circle of stars in the national flag's canton, and, elongated into a rectangle, begun service as the South's naval jack. As the storm flag of the sloop-of-war *Shenandoah*, the A.N.V.-pattern circumnavigated the globe in 1864 and 1865. (It would pull similar duty 120 years later when carried into orbit aboard an enemy U.S. space shuttle.) Confederate soldiers loved the battle flag and relinquished it only under duress, with many regiments preferring to burn theirs rather than surrender them. Such immolation took place on the way to Appomattox despite the "crown" of red flags that Chamberlain saw passing there—flags that heralded the sublime moment when honor was answered in kind.

"She Spurned the Yankee Scum"

Belle Boyd began doing so at age 17, when, according to her own account, she shot a Federal soldier who dared to raise a U.S. flag over her Martinsburg, Virginia home. Most likely, this unfortunate Yank was dropped by Miss Boyd's hunting rifle just before he had a chance to fall in love with the future Confederate agent—but others weren't as lucky. Nor did Southern sympathies grant any immunity from her charms—for the skirted spy who helped Turner Ashby and Stonewall Jackson win the Shenandoah Valley Campaign seduced men freely without regard to their status as noxious Union dross.

While Miss Boyd's career in espionage involved repeated arrests, her allure invariably helped curtail the imprisonment that followed. Once a dastardly beau by the name of C.W.D. Smitely, a West Virginia cavalryman, betrayed her into Old Capital Prison. In what may have been a fit of displaced aggression, she furiously assailed the Federal detective chief, Lafayette Baker, who had the effrontery to suggest she sign a loyalty oath to the Union while there. "I hope that when I commence that oath," she swore instead, "my tongue may cleave to the

continued on page 175...

Telescope Tripod

An exact replica of that used by Union Gen. Albert Meyer's Signal Service. Meticulously replicated in oak by Stephen Alexander for its having been "a thing of beauty … unreproduced by anyone else."

Price: $300.

Second Empire Fine Furniture
2927 Guilford Avenue
Baltimore, MD 21218
Phone: 410-366-7244

Confederate Cipher Wheel

What are you doing to execute the instructions sent you to HCDL-VW XMWIQIG KM ... If success will be more certain you can substitute EJT-FKMPG OPGEEVT KQFARLF TAG HEEPZ-ZU BBWYPHDN OMOMNQQG.

—Jefferson Davis, in an 1864 message to Gen. Kirby Smith, commander of the Confederacy's Trans-Mississippi Department.

Because it was the first war in which the telegraph played an important role, the Civil War had a greater use for encoded military messages. While the telegraph significantly increased the speed and number of such messages that could be sent, the wires over which they traveled were never secure. Indeed, it was at a telegraph pole in the woods outside Petersburg, Virginia, where the spy Charles Gaston obtained information that enabled a Confederate raiding force to make off with 3,000 head of cattle en route to Grant.

The Confederate cipher wheel was operated in tandem with a method developed by the sixteenth-century French cryptographer Blaise de Vigenere. This system used a tableau of staggered alphabets (called the "Vicksburg Square" by the C.S.) in conjunction with a secret phrase to encipher and decode cryptic messages. Old as it was, this method was superior to the relatively simple transposition cipher the Union employed.

Using the secret phrase *Manchester Bluff,* Confederate code clerks created the "polyalphabetic substitutions" that President Davis, above, used to communicate with Gen. Smith. His message (which this computer's spell-checker partly translates as "Volkswagen jet heaps zoo") asked the general what he was doing to gain a foothold on the Mississippi's eastern bank. Sometime after Washington code-breakers deciphered the Manchester Bluff phrase, Southern encrypters switched to *Come Retribution* and *Complete Victory,* forcing the Union decoders to begin again from scratch.

Brass cipher wheels similar to those replicated in wood by Goodwin's were useful in helping clerks translate encrypted messages quickly and accurately.

Dimensions: Two cipher discs are available. The smaller, measuring 3¾ inches in diameter by ½ inch in depth, is made of poplar, red oak, or mahogany. The larger is made of mahogany and measures 5¾ inches in diameter by ¾ inch in depth.

Prices: Small size: poplar or red oak, $22.95; mahogany, $24.95. Large size: $34.95. Prices include domestic shipping.

Complete instructions attached.

Goodwin's
P.O. Box 456
Dover Plains, NY 12522
Phone: 914-877-6445

Yankee Scum, continued

roof of my mouth. If I ever sign one line to show allegiance, I hope my arms fall paralyzed to my side... Get out! I am so disgusted I can't endure your presence any longer."

This put Baker into full rout—and Boyd vigorously swept down her cell behind him just as she had done in the wake of soldiers who came to stop her singing the scornful line from "Maryland, My Maryland" that titles this sidebar. Although for the time being Boyd had to remain in prison, she did so as a Confederate cappi de tutti cappi—enjoying fashionable food and magazines in her parlor-like lock-up. Boyd's inevitable release sent her to Richmond a heroine while it imprisoned the heart of the jail's superintendent, who futilely sent a trousseau along after her.

A different fate awaited the femme fatale's next captor. Once trapped on a captured blockade-runner, Boyd so charmed the enemy vessel's young ensign that he too proposed and was recruited as a Confederate spy in return. The ensign's name was Sam Hardinge, and after it was discovered he betrayed his country, he followed Boyd to England. Their marriage there was one of the major events of the social season.

After the war, Hardinge returned to America where he was jailed as a Southern agent, dying soon after. His widow—then all of twenty-one—turned to lecturing and writing throughout the U.S. and England until her death in 1900. She lies buried in Wisconsin, beneath a headstone that proclaims her young life as a Confederate spy.

The C.S.S. *Alabama*

The Confederacy's fearsome ship was built for the Lairds of Liverpool shipyard. Measuring 220 feet stem to stern and 32 feet across her beam, the raider carried among her armaments a 110-pounder rifled gun, an 8-inch solid-shot gun and six 32-pounders. While she bore a full complement of sails, she was usually propelled by two 300-horsepower engines that operated a double-wheel.

The C.S.S. Alabama was the most famous of the Confederate commerce raiders that ever preyed upon Union merchantmen. Ignoring the fact that since 1819 there had been a Federal ship named Alabama in service, she was commissioned off the Azores on August 24, 1862. Her crew numbered 144 under the command of Capt. Raphael Semmes, a U.S. Naval officer who had begun the war as head of the Confederate Lighthouse Service. Semmes and his ship began her career with decimation of the Yankee whaling fleet in the Azores—destroying ten ships within a fortnight. The raider then traveled like a spark along a fuse, sailing for the whaling centers of Newfoundland and the coast of New England, where she captured eleven more enemy vessels, burning the ships after removing their crews and provisions. She then turned south, prowling the East Coast of the U.S. to the Caribbean before sailing, in January of '63, into the Gulf of Mexico. Near Galveston, Texas, she attacked and sunk the blockading U.S. warship Hatteras before wheeling her hull southward again to outrun pursuing Union warships. Along the coast of South America the Alabama would put even more Yankee ships to the torch before recrossing the Atlantic to the

continued on page 171...

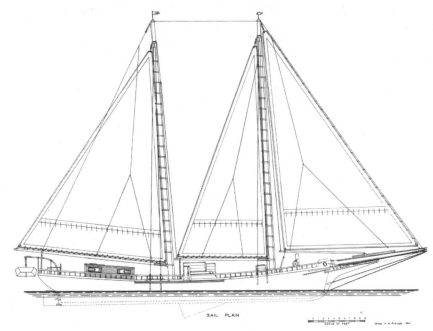

Sail Plan - G.W. Glenn

Ship Plans

Ship plans for the C.S.S. *Alabama* as well as those of many other Union and Confederate vessels are available from the National Watercraft Collection of the National Museum of American History. Derived primarily from the works of renowned naval historian H.I. Chapelle, these are available in two sets: *The Smithsonian Collection of Warship Plans,* and the 250-page *Ship Plan List of the Maritime Collection.* In the former, naval designs range from the mid-eighteenth to the early twentieth centuries, comprising vessels from the Continental, Confederate States, and United States Navies. *The Ship Plan List* contains design drawings of such varied and historical vessels as Columbus' flagship, the *Santa Maria;* the 1775 tobacco ship *Brilliant;* the Confederate blockade-runner C.S.S. *Fergus/Dare;* and fifteen Seattle fishing boats from the period extending from 1910 to 1930. In both collections, some vessels are represented by a single line drawing or inboard profile, while others—such as the original frigate *Constitution* or the Revolutionary War gunboat *Philadelphia*—are rendered in as many as sixteen sheets of drawings.

The C.S.S. Alabama

In addition to the *Alabama*, the *Warship Plans* catalog contains drawings for the C.S.S. *Albemarle*, the C.S.S. *Neuse* and *Arkansas*; the U.S.S. *Baron de Kalb* and *Cairo*, and the monitors *Camanche, Passaic, Camonicus,* and *Casco*, among others.

Income from the sale of the plan books goes toward making masters of older, more fragile drawings while furthering other aspects of the publication process.

Ship Plans
Smithsonian Institution
Division of Transportation
Room 5010 NMAH/MRC628
Washington, DC 20560

The U.S.S. Ironclad Cairo

The C.S.S. Alabama, continued

Cape of Good Hope. Now in the Indian Ocean en route to Asia, her reputation was enough to keep Union ships bound fast to their hawsers. The Alabama flew the Confederate naval jack in Singapore, India, and down the east coast of Africa before crossing the Atlantic again to South America.

Twenty-two months had passed and the U.S. government renamed their Alabama the U.S.S. New Hampshire. Badly in need of an overhaul, Capt. Semmes sailed the Confederate vessel into the port of Cherbourg, France, on June 11, 1864, having traveled 75,000 miles to take sixty-four Union ships without ever entering a Confederate port. The raider's exploits ended on Sunday the 19th, when she was sunk in combat with the U.S.S. Kearsarge. The contest took place in the English channel, from which Semmes was rescued by the British yacht Deerhound, which had sailed out for a good view. In postwar arbitration, the United States was awarded $15,500,000 in compensation from Great Britain for the damage inflicted by the Alabama.

Steam Launch

In April of 1864, Lieutenant William Barker Cushing learned that his friend, Commander Charles Flusser, was killed aboard the U.S.S. *Miami*. The *Miami* was the first ship to fall before the mighty *Albemarle*, a Confederate ram that appeared on the Roanoke River to recapture Plymouth, North Carolina, from the Federals. The *Albemarle* was built as a successor to the dreaded *Merrimack*, and her 160 feet of two-inch iron plate and main battery of six cannon won her the solemn respect of the U.S. Navy Department. Cushing considered the destruction of this floating fortress a fitting way to avenge Comdr. Flusser's death, but he was unable to attract official support for the plan. Cushing therefore settled on the simple idea of sinking the *Albemarle* freelance—with a torpedo.

As he had no submarine, Cushing resolved to use a steam launch to deliver the weapon affixed to a forward-mounted spar. Anticipating the stealthy torpedo boats of both World Wars, he planned to use this craft to steal upon the *Albemarle* by night and strike her below the water line.

That October, while the *Albemarle* was anchored off Plymouth, word came to one of her officers, Alexander F. Warley, that a steam launch had been seen on the river. This rumor must have increased Warley's unease on the "dark and slightly rainy" night of October 27, when he doubled the watch aboard the ram and alternated his pince-nez with binoculars in an effort to pierce the darkness enveloping her hull. Then, sometime after 11, Warley saw a bizarre silhouette approach. It was Lt. Cushing steaming down upon the *Albemarle* in his oddly-armed launch.

Cushing had just eluded pickets aboard the wrecked *Southfield*, and was now "within hailing distance," according to his mate, Thomas S. Gay. Confirming this, the launch was then hailed by the *Albemarle*. "We made no answer," Gay wrote. "We were hailed again, making no answer, but still getting in a fairer position."

Cushing blowing up the Albemarle.

His fears of an attack fulfilled, Warley wildly rang the *Albemarle's* alarm, but with Cushing's launch in too close for the ram's main guns to be trained on her, he was forced to rely on a less effective counterstrike. Warley issued an order for all hands to fire their muskets at the small boat, and for a storm of grape to pour down on her from the *Albemarle's* rear gun.

Undeterred by the barrage, Cushing continued to steer for "the dark mountain of iron in front of us." The torpedo boat was hailed again—this time by James W. Cooke, the *Albemarle's* captain, a Goliath demanding to know the David threatening him. Cushing, his coat now torn out by buckshot, answered with a dose of canister from the launch's howitzer and a demand of his own: "Leave the ram," he warned the *Albemarle* from the murk below, "or I'll blow you to pieces."

Cushing's diary continues: "We were near enough then, and I ordered the boom to be lowered until the forward motion of the launch carried the torpedo under the ram's overhang. A strong pull of the detaching line, a moment's waiting for the torpedo to rise under the hull, and I hauled in the left hand, just cut by a bullet. The explosion took place at the same instant that 100 pounds of grape, at 10 feet range, crashed among us and the dense mass of water thrown out by the torpedo came down with choking weight upon us." With a hole in her side that Warley described as "big enough to drive a wagon in," the *Albemarle* was going down for good.

Cooke twice ordered his attackers to surrender, but Cushing hollered for them to save themselves instead. Then, throwing his gear overboard, Cushing leapt into the river and, after a long and arduous passage in which he saw shipmates die, he made his way back to the Federal fleet.

Although the Medal of Honor was—mysteriously—not forthcoming, Lt. Cushing received the thanks of both the Navy

Department and Congress for his daring raid. However, in the end he may have derived more satisfaction from Alexander Warley's portrait of the assault as the most gallant of the war; and more still from the fact that, as a result of his bravery, the death of Charles W. Flusser was spectacularly avenged.

While it's difficult to imagine it transporting Cushing's torpedo, word of Beckmann Limited's replica of the 1905 *Compromise*—a 21 foot, general-purpose steam launch—comes to us with the notation that it is "similar and the same as launches built during the 1860s."

The *Compromise's* name refers to the efforts that the launch's original maker made in perfecting the hull pattern of previous models. To replicate the craft, the Beckmann company fashioned a mold from an original, ninety-two-year old Truscott hull. The launch can swing a 20-inch-diameter propeller and accepts a wide range of standard power plants with boiler requirements in the two- to four- horsepower range. These include vertical fire tube and horizontal water tube boilers fired by wood, coal or fuel oil.

Prices: $3,950, the bare hull. Steam-away versions of the *Compromise,* complete with power plant, propulsion train and woodwork, are available for $19,450.

Literature on replica launches and tugboats available.

Beckmann Limited
P.O. Box 97
Wakefield, RI 02880-0097
Phone and Fax: 401-783-1859
Boat Shop: 401-294-1030

Rum Measure

In July 1862 the U.S. Congress outlawed issuance of a "spirit ration" to Union seaman—a tradition that had extended back to the eighteenth century. However, when U.S., British, or Confederate sailors did sidle up to the ship's purser at the scuttlebutt to receive their quarter-gill of spirits—whether whiskey or rum—it was often taken in handmade copper cups such as the one depicted. With a height of two inches, these were standard in size and a regular part of the Navy outfit.

Price: $12.

Trading Stories
P.O. Box 604
Cottage Grove, OR 97424
Phone: 800-895-3050

Santa Claus

The historical Jesus was born in Bethlehem around the time that Judea was being divided among King Herod's sons. The American Santa was born nearly two millenia later—on the cover of *Harper's Weekly* just after Vicksburg came under attack by Gen. Sherman's troops.

Like Sherman, this Thomas Nast Santa was distinctly pro-Union in his sympathies. If a viewer doubted this after seeing him depicted visiting Federal soldiers in a sleigh loaded past the gunwales with presents—they needed only look farther in the drawing to witness the patriotically dressed Claus entertaining troops by hanging a Jeff Davis doll.

An expert on the subject, Kevin Rawlings is well aware that Thomas Nast used Santa for political purposes and to "convey a national spirit." Mr. Rawlings annually dons the red-striped trousers, red stocking cap and star-studded coat of Nast's Santa to lecture on Christmas during the Civil War. Upheld in this effect by a pair of knee-high black boots and the beard that the forty-year-old member of the Fourteenth Tennessee Volunteer Infantry begins growing out each July, Rawlings is a singular spectacle of nineteenth-century reenactment. Through appearances made at national battlefields and historic sites in the Mid-Atlantic region, and—more broadly—through his recent book on the subject, Rawlings has thereby made a gift of his love for both the histories of Christmas and the War Between the States.

HARPER'S WEEKLY.

A JOURNAL OF CIVILIZATION

Vol. VII.—No. 314.]　　　NEW YORK, SATURDAY, JANUARY 3, 1863.　　　[SINGLE COPIES SIX CENTS.
$4 00 PER YEAR IN ADVANCE.

SANTA CLAUS IN CAMP.—[See Page 6.]

For information regarding appearances by the Civil War Santa Claus, contact:

Kevin Rawlings
P.O. Box 389
Sharpsburg, MD 21782
Phone: 301-432-7019

Copies of Mr. Rawlings' *We Were Marching on Christmas Day: A History and Chronicle of Christmas During the Civil War* are available for $24.95 hard cover, and $19.95, soft cover.

Toomey's Bookshop
P.O. Box 122
Linthicum, MD 21090
Phone or Fax:
410-850-0831

Coffin

Lee's surrender of the Army of Northern Virginia to Grant at Appomattox took place on April 9, 1865. But the Civil War wasn't over yet. On May 12, Confederate troops under Col. John S. Ford repulsed a force led by Col. Theodore H. Barrett in a clash known as the Battle of Palmito Ranch—the war's last serious land action. Shortly after, Confederate Gen. Kirby Smith disbanded the last Confederate army in the field when he surrendered 43,000 troops of the Trans-Mississippi Department at Galveston. On June 22, the Confederate commerce raider *Shenandoah,* commanded by Capt. James I. Waddell, captured the Northern whaler *Jerah Swift* in the Bering Sea with a round from her Whitworth cannon—the war's last shot. Then, on November 6, the same Capt. Waddell lowered the Confederate colors for the last official time aboard the *Shenandoah* as she lay at anchor in Liverpool, England.

But these events only ended the shooting. For more than 130 years now, others have marked a continuing Civil War history in which Appomattox was only a pause to water the horses.

In the Reconstruction South there was the rise of the Ku Klux Klan and Lost Cause Movements. Then, in a more conciliatory spirit, came the twentieth century's blue and gray veteran's reunions. In the 1930s, the Atlanta premiere of "Gone With the Wind" indicated a greatly revived interest in the Civil War-era South; and the Dixiecrat insurgency at the Democratic National Convention nine years later invoked rhetoric that was positively *Confederate* in nature.

Capping the early civil rights movement, the admission of African-Americans into the University of Alabama provoked a display of battle flags and soldiers in battle dress to threaten a Civil War reenactment of terrible authenticity; while at the 1968 March on Washington, Martin Luther King's recitation of "The Battle Hymn of the Republic" reinforced militancy with piety for a second century. Most poignantly, during the 1960s the Civil War lived on in her oldest veterans, the last of whom, a Confederate, died just before the Civil War's Centennial.

Also vivid is the more recent history of the American Civil War. It includes the 1989 flying of the Confederate battle flag by revolutionaries in the streets of Prague and at the Berlin Wall; the protest against the Southern use of that same banner during the 1996 Atlanta Olympics; the combative work of battlefield preservation groups; Ken Burns' eponymous PBS television series and its haunting theme "Ashokan Farewell"—perhaps the most beautiful Civil War replica ever wrought; the soldiers and sutlers at blue-gray reenactments; the film "Gettysburg" and the undying popular regard for Abraham Lincoln, Jefferson Davis, and Robert E. Lee, among their honorable cohorts.

The Civil War also survives in this moment, upheld by this and the many other books published about the unforgettable conflict and—more importantly—by those who read them. It survives even in those who hate the whole business and wish it would just fade away. You can buy a full-sized replica of the Civil War's coffin, dear reader, but the war itself will never die.

"Price List-Order Form" available.

Bert & Bud's Vintage Coffins
Route 7, Box 138
Murray, KY 42071
Phone: 502-753-9279

In their portrayals of history significant to the Civil War, the following historic(al) sites each employ living history interpreters and / or programs.

1816-1829
Lincoln Living Historical Farm

Lincoln City, IN 47552
Phone: 812-937-4541
Fax: 812-937-9929

The Lincoln Living Historical Farm features a typical 1820s log cabin similar to the one that sheltered Lincoln when he was a boy. A smokehouse, chicken house, stable, and workshop complete the site. Period crops are cultivated in the fields. Open daily from mid-April through October.

1830s
Lincoln's New Salem State Historic Site

R.R. 1 Box 244A
Petersburg, IL 62675
Phone: 217-632-4000
Fax: 217-632-4010

A 620-acre re-creation of the Illinois village where Abraham Lincoln lived at the beginning of his political career, from 1831 to 1837. It was here where Lincoln claimed to have grown from an "aimless piece of driftwood" into a lawyer while trying his hand at storekeeping, surveying, soldiering (Lincoln was a militia captain in the Black Hawk War) and flatboat piloting along the way. Situated two miles south of Petersburg on Illinois 97, New Salem's forested surroundings reinforce the the staff's first-person interpretation with the illusion of a frontier environment. Open daily, save for major holidays.

1840s
Lincoln Log Cabin State Historic Site

R.R. 1 Box 175
Lerna, IL 62440
Phone: 217-345-6489

A detailed reproduction of the log cabin (actually a large, southern-style "saddlebag" house) that Abraham Lincoln's father and stepmother occupied from 1840 until their deaths in 1851 and 1869 respectively. The house, which sheltered eighteen members of the extended Lincoln family and was occasionally visited by Abraham, itself journeyed to the Chicago Columbian Exposition in 1891. Lincoln Log Cabin uses a living-history interpretation of the year 1845 and has developed more than 100 historical characters who appear in various combinations throughout the year.

1860s
Meadow Farm Museum

General Sheppard Crump Memorial Park
County of Henrico
Division of Recreation and Parks
P.O. Box 27032
Richmond, VA 23273
Phone: 804-672-5520

The Meadow Farm, owned by the Sheppard family from 1713 to 1983, is the setting for the re-creation of events of 1860, when Dr. John Sheppard ran the farm with his wife and nine children. First-person events include "Civil War Days," a September Civil War reenactment, and a "Yuletide Feast," coincident with a December encampment. Open daily except Monday, the museum is closed during January and February.

Shiloh National Military Park

Shiloh, TN 38376
Phone: 901-689-5275
Fax: 901-689-5450

A 4,000-acre park situated 110 miles east of Memphis, Shiloh National Military Park documents the failure of Generals Albert Sidney Johnston (who was killed in the battle) and P.G.T. Beauregard to halt Grant's seizure of Confederate railroads during the bloody fighting of April 6 and 7, 1862. Occasional living history programs are offered in the park, which has a Visitors' Center, bookstore, and small museum. Open daily from 8 a.m. to 5 p.m. except between Memorial and Labor Days, when it remains open until 6 p.m. Closed on Christmas.

Federal cavalrymen hasten to the front during Shiloh on April 6, 1862.

Wilson's Creek National Battlefield

6424 West Farm Road 182
Republic, MO 65738-0403
Phone: (417) 732-2662

The August to November 1861 Wilson's Creek campaign, in which Confederates commanded by Gen. Sterling Price undertook to gain control of Missouri was one of the first significant military campaigns of the war. Wilson's Creek National Battlefield is situated on 1,750 acres, three miles east of Republic, Missouri. It offers a 4.9-mile self-guided tour including Bloody Hill, where 4,000 troops under U.S. Gen. Nathaniel Lyon held the high ground against repeated attacks in one of the most fiercely contested engagements of the war. On summer weekends, living history demonstrations are offered there and at the Ray House, which was used as a Confederate field hospital during the campaign. The park is open from 8 a.m. to 7 p.m., every day except Christmas and New Year's.

Old Bethpage Village Restoration

Round Swamp Road
Old Bethpage, NY 11804
Phone: 516-572-8401
Fax: 516-572-8413

Located forty miles east of New York City, Old Bethpage recreates the folklife of a Long Island farm community of the 1850s. Each year, hundreds of reenactors participate in the unique re-creation of a Civil War training camp at the village.

Heritage Hill

2640 South Webster Avenue
Green Bay, WI 54301
Phone: 800-721-5150

Overlooking the Fox River in Green Bay, Wisconsin, Heritage Hill's living history exhibits are thematically grouped to represent four periods in the state's history: pioneer heritage, Belgian colonization, early nineteenth-century military life, and the mid-Victorian period, or 1870s. In June, the museum hosts a Civil War encampment complete with band concert and a military ball.

Richmond National Battlefield Park

3215 Broad Street
Richmond, VA 23223
Phone: 804-226-1981
Fax: 804-771-8522

Located on 770 acres, the Richmond National Battlefield Park offers a 100-mile self-guided tour of sites significant to the Richmond campaigns of 1862 and 1864. Living history programs are offered at Cold Harbor, Fort Harrison, Drewry's Bluff, and Malverne Hill throughout the year. The Visitors' Center is open from 9 a.m. to 5 p.m., every day except Christmas and New Year's. Grounds are open from dawn until dusk.

Cumberland Gap National Historic Park

Middlesboro, KY 40965
Phone: 606-248-2817
Fax: 606-248-7276

A Visitors' Center contains a museum of the Cumberland Gap, which was a strategic objective during the Civil War and changed hands several times. The Gap was captured on June 18, 1862 by Union Gen. George W. Morgan, who withdrew the following September, following the Confederate army's invasion of Kentucky. On September 9, 1863, Union forces recaptured the Gap. Occasional living history programs are presented. The Visitors' Center is open from 8 a.m. to 5 p.m. daily except for Thanksgiving, Christmas, New Year's, Martin Luther King's Birthday and President's Day.

Kennesaw Mountain National Battlefield Park

900 Kennesaw Mountain Drive
Kennesaw, GA 30152
Phone: 770-427-4686
Fax: 770-427-1760

The battle of Kennesaw Mountain was part of the Atlanta Campaign that began on May 5, 1864 and pitted troops under the command of Confederate Gen. Joseph Johnston against the army of 100,000 led by William Tecumseh Sherman. The fight, which took place early on June 27, provided Sherman with substantiation for his rule that "whichever party attacked first got the worst of it" when he was repulsed on all points by Johnston. The Kennesaw Mountain National Battlefield is situated three miles north of Marietta and offers a self-guided tour that begins at the Visitors' Center and includes an observation point close to the summit that provides a sweeping view of the battle's terrain. Living history programs are presented throughout the summer. The park is open daily save for Christmas, when the Visitors' Center is closed.

Kennesaw Mountain

Petersburg National Battlefield

1539 Hickory Hill Road
Petersburg, VA 23803-4721
Phone: 804-732-3531
Fax: 804 732-3615

The Petersburg National Battlefield occupies roughly 2,700 acres where for ten months between June of 1864 and April of 1865, U.S. Grant lay siege to this city, which he regarded as "the key to taking Richmond." The park comprises a Visitors' Center, Grant's headquarters at City Point, the Five Forks Battlefield, many fortifications and batteries, and the Poplar Grove National Cemetery. Beginning in June of 1996, summertime living history demonstrations of the lives of Civil War soldiers will take place on a trial basis for an entry fee of $7 per person. The park is open 8 a.m. to dark, every day except Christmas and New Year's and certain winter holidays, including Martin Luther King's birthday.

In the trenches before Petersburg, Union soldiers await their officers' assessment of a Confederate position.

Appomattox Court House National Historical Park

P.O. Box 218
Appomattox, VA 24522
Phone: 804-352-8782
Fax: 804-352-8330

The Appomattox Court House National Park occupies 1,326 acres on a site located fourteen miles east of Lynchburg, Virginia. Summertime living history demonstrations portray the daily life of villagers during the war. In addition to Meeks' Store, the Courthouse and "Surrender Triangle," the park contains the McLean House, in the parlor of which Gen. Lee surrendered the Army of Northern Virginia on April 9, 1865. Open 8:30 a.m. to 5:00 p.m. between Memorial and Labor Days, then 9:00 to 5:30.

Robert E. Lee signs the instrument of surrender as Ulysses S. Grant and others look on in the McLean house at Appomattox Court house, Virginia, on April 9, 1865. Several of the Union officers depicted were not actually present.

CIVIL WAR REENACTMENT GROUPS

The following reenactment organizations are arranged according to their status as Federal, Confederate, and combined groups—the last category containing member units from both sides.

Much of this information was obtained through the courtesy of Camp Chase Publishing Company.

Federal Organizations

Cumberland Guard
Indiana, Illinois, Ohio, Michigan and Kentucky.
Contact: David Shackelford
P.O. Box 20276
Indianapolis, IN 46220

Frontier Battalion
Arkansas, Oklahoma, Nebraska,
Illinois, Iowa, Missouri, Indiana.
Contact: Mark Dolive
2060 Paint Pony
Keller, TX 76248

Mifflin Guard
New York, New Jersey, Pennsylvania, Delaware.
Contact: Scott Washburn
13460 Trevose Road
Philadelphia, PA 19116-1707

Second Corps
Virginia, Maryland, Pennsylvania,
New Jersey, Delaware.
Contact: Jack Pickett
116 West Main Street
Middletown, DE 19709

U. S. Volunteers
New Jersey, Maryland, New York, Pennsylvania
Delaware, Virginia, North Carolina, South Carolina,
Ohio, West Virginia, Connecticut, Massachusetts,
New Hampshire, Vermont, Maine.
Contact: Dana Heim
8 Wintermere Road
Lebanon, PA 17042

Union Army, District of Florida
Florida.
Contact: Jeff Grzelak
7214 Laurel Hill Road
Orlando, FL 32818

Union Rifles
Oklahoma, Missouri, Arkansas, Mississippi.
Contact: Cal Kinzer
2026 E. 140th Place South
Bixby, OK 74008-3657

Vincent's Brigade
Maryland, Pennsylvania, New Jersey, Delaware.
Contact: Wayne Wolff
604 Friar Tuck Road
Belair, MD 21014

Western Brigade
Kentucky, Illinois, Indiana, Ohio, Michigan,
Minnesota, Missouri, New York, Wisconsin.
Contact: Don Heitman
2909 East 62nd Street
Indianapolis, IN 46220

Confederate Organizations

Army of Northern Virginia
Virginia, New York, Pennsylvania,
New Jersey, Maryland, West Virginia,
North Carolina, Delaware, Tennessee, Georgia.
Contact: Don Patterson
1703 Carver Square
Salisbury, MD 21801

Confederate Military Force
Virginia, Maryland, Pennsylvania.
Contact: George Heffner
P.O. Box 88
Clarksburg, MD 20871

Department of the Gulf
Florida.
Contact: Don Bowman
34740 Chancey Road
Zephyr Hills, FL 33541

First Confederate Division: 1st Brigade
Texas, Tennessee, Arkansas, Ohio, Indiana, West
Virginia, Kentucky, Illinois, Mississippi, California,
Michigan, Missouri, Florida, Louisiana, New Mexico.
Contact: Al Gatlin
10602 Trousdale Ferry Pike
Lebanon, TN 37090

First Confederate Division: 2nd Brigade:
Alabama, Texas, Arkansas, Tennessee, Louisiana,
Mississippi, Oklahoma, South Carolina, Kansas,
Missouri.
Contact: Bill Smart
355 Mohawk Road
Big Cove, AL 35763-9251

Georgia Division
Georgia.
Contact: Frank L. Benson, Jr.
6108 Tracy Valley Drive
Norcross, GA 30093-2030

Jackson's Division
Virginia.
Contact: Floyd Bayne
14407 Huntgate Woods Road
Midlothian, VA 23112

Longstreet's Division
Virginia, Maryland, North Carolina.
Contact: George F. Miller
28 Teton Drive
Fredericksburg, VA 22401

North Carolina Battalion
North Carolina, South Carolina, Tennessee, Virginia.
Contact: Jeff Stepp
Nathan Drive
Arden, NC 28704

Confederate commissary headquarters, Living History Museum, Hogback Mountain Vermont.

Both Federal & Confederate

Armies of the Tennessee
Illinois, Indiana, Kentucky, Ohio, Tennessee.
Contact: Gen. Mickey M. Walker
P.O. Box 91
Rosedale, IN 47874

The Living History Association
United States and Canada
Contact: James Dassatti
Box 1589
Wilmington, VT 05363

Missouri Civil War Reenactors Association
Arkansas, Missouri, Illinois, Kansas, Nebraska.
Contact: David Kesinger
142 SE 411
Warrensburg, MO 64093

The National Civil War Association
California, Nevada, Oregon, Washington.
Contact: Roy H. Wells
P.O. Box 70084
Sunnyvale, CA 94806

New England artillery fires into advancing Confederates at the Living History Association's annual Civil War Days.

Southern California Civil War Association

Arizona, California, Oregon.
Contact: Gary Fradella
13319 Branding Iron Place
Chino, CA 91710-4706

Union & Confederate Volunteers

Connecticut, Maine, Massachusetts, New Hampshire,
Vermont, New York, Georgia.
Contact: Steven C. Huddleston, Deborah Wetmore
12 Bow Street
Danvers, MA 01923-3520

West Virginia Reenactor's Association

West Virginia, Virginia, Ohio.
Contact: Peter Baxter
199 Summit Street
Elkins, WV 26241

10th Massachussetts Volunteer Infantry advances during the Living History Association's annual Civil War Days.

SUPPLIERS

A. Lincoln's Place
66
460 Baltimore Street
Gettysburg, PA 17325
Phone: 717-334-6049

Amazon Drygoods
42, 46, 49, 59-60, 91
2218 E. 11th Street
Davenport, IA 52803-3760
Phone: 319-322-6800
Fax: 319-322-4003
Order Line: 800-798-7979

American Forests
16-17
8555 Plummer Road
Jacksonville, FL 32219
Phone: 904-765-0727

Antique Doll Reproductions
62
R.R. 1, Box 103
Milo, MO 64767
Phone: 417-876-4785
417-876-6280 (summers)

Authentic Reproductions
170
1031 Old Nankin Road, R-3
Ashland, OH 44805
Phone: 419-289-6642
or 419-289-8688
Fax: 419-289-8688

Beckmann Limited
178-179
P.O. Box 97
Wakefield, RI 02880-0097
Phone & Fax: 401-783-1859
Boat Shop: 401-294-1030

Bert & Bud's Vintage Coffins
181
Route 7, Box 138
Murray, KY 42071
Phone: 502-753-9279

Peter Blaisdell
64-65
P.O. Box 725
Naples, NY 14512
Phone: 716-374-9282

Border States Leatherworks
153, 158, 166
1158 Apple Blossom Lane
Springdale, AR 72762
Phone: 501-361-2642
Fax: 501-361-2851

Broadfoot Publishing Company
55-57
1907 Buena Vista Circle
Wilmington, NC 28405
Phone: 910-686-4816
Fax: 910-686-4379
Order Line: 800-537-5243

The Carpetbagger
52-53
7805 Main Street
Middletown, VA 22645
Phone: 540-869-7732

Cartridges Unlimited
81, 89, 130
4320-A Hartford Street
St. Louis, MO 63116
Phone: 314-664-4332

Cavalry Regimental Supply
149
Box 64394
Lubbock, TX 79464
Fax: 806-798-8867

Cavalry Shop
120, 159, 164, 166-167
9700 Royerton Drive
Richmond, VA 23228
Phone: 804-266-0898

Chadsworth's 1.800.Columns
20-21
P.O. Box 2618
Wilmington, NC 28402
Phone: 800-COLUMNS
Fax: 910-763-3191
In Atlanta, phone: 876-5410

Civil War Trust
16-17
1225 Eye Street, N.W.
Suite 401
Washington, DC 20005
Phone: 202-326-8420
Fax: 202-408-5679

Classic Portraits Fine Arts
67
4 Marshs Victory Court
Baltimore, MD 21228
Phone: 410-747-8780
For orders : 800-677-3257

Clearwater Hat Company
41, 147-148
Box 202
Newnata, AR 72680
Phone: 501-746-4324

Commonwealth Vintage Dancers
63
99 Malvern Street
Melrose, MA 02176
Phone: 617-396-2870

Confederate Treasury Company
61
1100 North Main Street
Tennessee Ridge, TN 37178
Phone: 615-721-3301
Fax: 615-721-4155
Order Line: 800-632-2383

County Cloth
72, 150
13797-C Georgetown Street, N.E.
Paris, OH 44669
Phone: 330-862-3307
Fax: 330-862-3304

Crazy Crow Trading Post
103
P.O. Box 314-AMS
Denison, TX 75020
Phone: 903-786-2287

Great American Pattern Emporium
43, 47
341 Mooreland Avenue
Harrodsburg, KY 40330
Phone: 606-734-0028

Green's Carriage Restoration & Heritage Museum
151
10530 Thrailkill Road
Orient, OH 43146
Phone: 614-877-4254
Fax: 614-983-2566

Hamilton Dry Goods
155
2510 Randolph Road
Cookeville, TN 38506
Phone: 615-528-6061

Heartland House
154-155, 158, 159
Old Blue Ridge Turnpike
Rochelle, VA 22738
Phone & Fax: 540-672-9267

Heirloom Reproductions
23
1834 W. Fifth Street
Montgomery, AL 36106-1516
Phone: 334-263-3511
Fax: 334-263-3313
Order line: 800-288-1513

Historical Replications, Inc.
18-19
P.O Box 13529
Dept. CW
Jackson, MS 39236
Phone: 800-426-5628
In MS: 601-981-8743

House of Kirk
106, 131
9380 Collins Parkway
P.O. Box 808
New Market, VA 22844
Phone: 540-740-8296
Fax: 540-740-4459

J.R. Burrows & Company
28
P. O. Box 522
393 Union Street
Rockland, MA 02370
Phone: 617-982-1812
Fax: 617-982-1636

The Jeweler's Daughter
50-51
2-4 W. Washington Street
Hagerstown, MD 21740
Phone: 301-733-3200
Fax: 301-733-5076

Kentwood Sutlery and Manufacturing
27, 75, 81, 101
P.O. Box 88201
Kentwood, MI 49518
Phone: 616-531-7645

Landis Valley Museum
80-81
Heirloom Seed Project
2451 Kissel Hill Road
Lancaster, PA 17601
Phone: 717-569-0401

Legendary Arms, Inc.
94, 132, 133
P.O. Box 29
Dunellen, NJ 08812-0299
Phone: 908-424-8636
Fax: 908-424-2303
Order line: 800-528-2767

Lehman's
22
P.O. Box 41
Kidron, OH 44636
Phone: 216-857-5757
Fax: 216-857-5785

M. Marsh & Son
102-103
915 Market Street
P.O. Box 6604
Wheeling, WV 26003
Phone: 800-624-5495
Fax: 304-232-4472

Martin's Mercantile
34, 38-39, 48
4566 Oakhurst Drive
Sylvania, OH 43560-1736
Phone & Fax: 419-474-2093

McIlhenny Company
83
Avery Island, LA 70513
Phone: 800-634-9599

Mechanical Baking Company
78
P.O. Box 513
Pekin, IL 61555-0513
Phone: 309-353-2414

Montana Boot Company
149
P.O. Box 77
Livingston, MT 59047
Phone: 406-222-7723

Moultrie Manufacturing Company
26
P.O. Drawer 1179
1403 Georgia Highway 133 South
Moultrie, GA 31776-1179
Phone: 800-841-8674

Mt. Diablo Handprints
30-31
940 Tyler Street # 56
P.O. Box 726
Benicia, CA 94510
Phone: 707-745-3388
Fax: 707-745-1726

Navy Arms Company
121-123, 126-127, 129, 133
689 Bergen Boulevard
Ridgefield, NJ 07657
Phone: 201-945-2500
Fax: 201-945-6859
Order Desk. 800-669-NAVY

Norman Publishing
92-93
720 Market Street
San Francisco, CA 94102-2502
Phone: 415-781-6402
Order Line: 800-544-9359
E-mail: orders@jnorman.com

Panther Primitives
70-71, 76, 77, 98, 107, 150
P.O. Box 32
Normantown, WV 25267
Phone: 304-462-7718
Order line: 800-487-2684

Past Patterns
44-46
P.O. Box 7587
Grand Rapids, MI 49510-7587
Phone: 616-245-9456
Fax: 616-245-3584

Peter Evans Pipes
105-106
285 West Mashta Drive
Dept. W
Key Biscayne, FL 33149
Phone: 305-361-5589

R&K Sutlery
32
1015-1200th Street
Lincoln, IL 62656
Phone: 217-732-8844

Kevin Rawlings
180
P.O. Box 389
Sharpsburg, MD 21782
Phone: 301-432-7019

**Red Willow Clothing
and Canvas Shelters**
70-71
Box 188
131 West Main Street
Oxford, IA 52322
Phone: 319-628-4815

Ronniger's Potatoes
82
Star Route
Moyie Springs, ID 83845
Phone: 208-267-7938
Fax: 208-267-3265

Saxton's Coronet Band
95
341 Mooreland Avenue
Harrodsburg, KY 40330
Phone: 606-734-0028

Schneider Enterprises
119
1252 N. Brownslake Road
Burlington, WI 53105-9794
Phone & Fax: 414-534-6813

Second Empire Fine Furniture
75, 174
2927 Guilford Avenue
Baltimore, MD 21218
Phone: 410-366-7244

Seed Savers Exchange
80-81
3076 North Winn Road
Decorah, IA 52101
Phone & Fax: 319-382-5872

**Silver Sunbeam
Photographic Gallery**
112-113
P.O. Box 269
Reserve, LA 70084
Phone: 504-535-8629

Smithsonian Institution
176
Division of Transportation
Room 5010 NMAH/MRC 628
Washington, DC 20560

South Bend Replicas, Inc.
117-118
61650 Oak Road
South Bend, IN 46614
Phone: 219-289-4500

Spectacle Accoutrements
110
2918 North Rolling Road
Baltimore, MD 21244
Phone: 410-281-6069

Steen Cannons
117-118
10730 Midland Trail Road
Cannonsburg, KY 41120
Phone & Fax: 606-329-2477

StereoType
62
P.O. Box 1637
Florence, OR 97439
Phone: 503-997-8879

Toomey's Bookshop
180
P.O. Box 122
Linthicum, MD 21090
Phone & Fax: 410-850-0831

Trading Stories
179
P.O. Box 604
Cottage Grove, OR 97424
Phone: 800-895-3050

Tremont Nail Company
19
8 Elm Street
P.O. Box 111
Wareham, MA 02571
Phone: 508-295-0038

U.S. Games Systems
100-101
179 Ludlow Street
Stamford, CT 06902
Phone: 203-353-8400
Fax: 203-353-8431
Order line: 800-544-2637

Uberti USA Inc.
125
P.O. Box 469
Lakeville, CT 06039
Phone: 860-435-8068
& 860-435-2846
Fax: 860-435-8146
E-mail. uberti@li.com

Village Tinsmithing Works
77, 84-86, 90, 111, 165
P.O. Box 189
Randolph, OH 44265
Phone: 330-325-9101

Wilkins-Rogers, Inc.
79
P.O. Box 308
Ellicott City, MD 21041
Phone: 410-465-5800

Wisconsin Veterans Museum
72
30 W. Mifflin Street
Madison, WI 53703
Phone: 608-266-1680

Woolrich, Inc.
73
Woolrich, PA 17779
Phone: 717-769-6464
Order line: 800-995-1299

Wunder Banjo Company
98-99
Phone: 800-891-6541

John A. Zaharias, Sutler
86
P.O. Box 31152
St. Louis, MO 63131
Phone: 314-966-2829
Order line: 800-966-2829

BIBLIOGRAPHY

Books

Batty, Peter and Parish, Peter. *The Divided Union.* Topsfield, Massachusetts: Salem House, 1987.

Bearss, Edwin C. *The Civil War Battlefield Guide.* Edited by Frances H. Kennedy. Arlington, Virginia: Houghton Mifflin, 1990.

Benét, Stephen Vincent. *John Brown's Body.* Reprint. Chicago, Ivan R. Dee, 1990.

Boatner, Mark M., III. *The Civil War Dictionary.* New York: Vintage Civil War Library, 1991.

Botkin, B.A., ed., *A Civil War Treasury of Tales, Legends, and Folklore, Recollections of Private Carlton McCarthy.* New York: Random House, 1960.

Bowman, John S., ed. *The Civil War Almanac.* New York: W.H. Smith. Gallery Books, 1983.

Cannon, Devereaux D., Jr. *The Flags of the Confederacy.* Gretna, Louisiana: Pelican Publishing Company, 1994.

Carruth, Gorton. *What Happened When.* New York: Signet Books, 1991.

Cash, W.J. *The Mind of the South,* 1941. Reprint. New York: Vintage Books, 1965.

Criswell, Grover C. III. *Col. Grover Criswell's Guide to Confederate Money.* Salt Springs, Florida: Criswell's Publications, 1991.

Daniel, Clifton. *Chronicle of America.* New York: Dorling Kindersley, 1995.

Davenport, Millia. *The Book of Costume.* New York: Crown Publishers, Inc., 1976.

Davis, Burke. *Our Incredible Civil War.* New York: Holt, Rhinehart and Winston, 1960.

Davis, Kenneth C. *Don't Know Much About the Civil War.* New York: Wm. Morrow & Co., 1996.

Downey, Fairfax. *Cannonade.* Garden City, New York: Doubleday & Co., 1966.

Drickhamer, Karen D. and Lee C., eds. Harpers Ferry: *On the Border of North and South with "Rambling Jour" A Civil War Soldier.* Shippensburg, Pennsylvania: White Mane Publishing Company, 1987.

Dupuy, R. Ernest and Trevor N. *The Compact History of the Civil War.* Reprint. New York: Warner Books, 1993.

Editors of Time-Life Books. *Arms and Equipment of the Confederacy.* New York: Time-Life Books, 1991.

Editors of Time-Life Books. *Arms and Equipment of the Union.* New York: Time-Life Books, 1991.

Ewing, Elizabeth. *Everyday Dress, 1660-1900.* New York: Chelsea House, 1984.

Foote, Shelby. *The Civil War.* 3 vols. New York: Vintage Books, 1986.

Freeman, D.S. *Lee's Lieutenants.* 3 vols. New York: Charles Scribner's Sons, 1942.

Fuller, Edmund, ed. *Bulfinch's Mythology.* Reprint. New York: Dell Publishing Company, 1959.

Gallagher, Gary W., ed. *Fighting for the Confederacy: The Personal Recollections of General Edward Porter Alexander.* Chapel Hill: University of North Carolina Press, 1989.

Garrison, Webb. *Civil War Curiosities.* Nashville: Rutledge Hill Press, 1994.

Garrison, Webb. *More Civil War Curiosities.* Nashville: Rutledge Hill Press, 1995.

Gowan, Judy and Hugh. *Blue and Grey Cookery.* Martinsburg, Pennsylvania: Daisy Publishing, 1980.

Gragg, Rod. *Civil War Quiz and Fact Book.* New York: Promontory Press, 1985.

Gragg, Rod. *The Illustrated Confederate Reader.* New York: Harper & Row, 1989.

Haythornthwaite, Philip. *Uniforms of the Civil War.* New York: Sterling Publishing Company, 1990.

Hoehling, A.A. *Damn the Torpedoes!: Naval Incidents of the Civil War.* Winston-Salem, North Carolina: J.F. Blair, 1989.

Kennedy, Roger G. *Greek Revival America.* New York: Stewart, Tabori & Chang, 1989.

Korn, Jerry. *Pursuit to Appomattox.* Alexandria: Time-Life Books, 1987.

Lacour-Gayet, Robert. *Everyday Life in the United States Before the Civil War,* 1830-1860. Translated by Mary Ilford from *La Vie quotidienne aux États-Unis, 1830-1860.* New York: Frederick Ungar Publishing Company, 1969.

Larkin, Jack. *The Reshaping of Everyday Life, 1790-1840.* The Everyday Life in America Series, edited by Richard Balkin. New York: Harper & Row, Perennial Library, 1989.

Lawliss, Chuck. *The Civil War Sourcebook: A Traveler's Guide.* New York: Harmony Books, 1991.

Leone, Mark P., and Silberman, Neal Asher. *Invisible America: Unearthing Our Hidden History.* New York: Henry Holt & Company, 1995.

Linn, Karen. *That Half-Barbaric Twang.* Urbana and Chicago: The University of Illinois Press, 1991.

Lord, Francis A. *The Civil War Collector's Encyclopedia.* Harrisburg, Pennsylvania: Stackpole Books, 1982.

Lord, Francis A. *They Fought for the Union.* Harrisburg, Pennsylvania: The Stackpole Company, 1960.

Lyman, Darryl. *Civil War Quotations.* Conshohocken, Pennsylvania: Combined Books, 1995.

McCarthy, Carlton. *Detailed Minutiae of Soldier Life in the Army of Northern Virginia, 1861-1865,* 1882. Reprint. Lincoln: Univerity of Nebraska Press, 1993.

McPherson, James M. *Abraham Lincoln and the Second American Revolution.* New York: Oxford University Press, 1990.

Mathews, Mitford, ed. *A Dictionary of Americanisms.* Chicago: University of Chicago Press, 1951.

Mitchell, Reid. *Civil War Soldiers.* New York: Touchstone Books, 1988.

Robertson, James I., *Soldiers in Blue & Gray.* New York: Warner Books, 1988.

Robertson, James I., and the Editors of Time-Life Books. *Tenting Tonight: The Soldier's Life.* New York: Time-Life Books, 1984.

Ward, Geoffrey C. *The Civil War: An Illustrated History.* New York: Alfred A. Knopf, Inc. 1990.

Wiley, Bell Irvin, and Milhollen, Hirst D. *They Who Fought Here.* New York: Bonanza Books, 1959.

Wright, Louis B. and Fowler, Elaine W. *Everyday Life in the New Nation, 1787-1860.* New York: G.P. Putnam's Sons, 1972.

Magazines

Antonucci, Michael. "Code-Crackers." *Civil War Times Illustrated,* August, 1995.

Boritt, Gabor S. "The President at Play" *Civil War Times Illustrated.* December, 1995.

Hodges, Robert R., Jr. "An Englishman's Journey Through the Confederacy." *America's Civil War,* July, 1996.

Holzer, Harold. "I Should Not Say Any Foolish Things." *Civil War Times Illustrated,* December, 1995.

O'Brien, Tom and Taylor, John. "Battle for the Rio Grande." *Civil War Times Illustrated,* October, 1995

INDEX

PHOTO CREDITS

All other illustrations and photographs were provided by product suppliers.

Overleaf: Confederate and Union Civil War veterans at the 50th anniversary of the Battle of Gettysburg.